IN SEARCH
OF WISDOM

In Search of Wisdom

Faith Formation in the Black Church

Edited by
Anne E. Streaty Wimberly
&
Evelyn L. Parker

Abingdon Press
Nashville

IN SEARCH OF WISDOM
FAITH FORMATION IN THE BLACK CHURCH

Library of Congress Cataloging-in-Publication Data

In search of wisdom : faith formation in the black church / edited by
Anne E. Streaty Wimberly, Evelyn L. Parker.
    p. cm.
Includes bibliographical references.
    ISBN 0-687-06700-6 (pbk. : alk. paper)
    1. Church work with African Americans.   2. African American churches.
3. African Americans—Religious life.   4. Christian
education—Biographical methods.   I. Wimberly, Anne Streaty, 1936–   II.
Parker, Evelyn L., 1953–
    BV4468.2.A34 I6 2002
    253'.089'96073—dc21

                                                                2002011920

02 03 04 05 06 07 08 09 10 11—10 9 8 7 6 5 4 3 2 1

MANUFACTURED IN THE UNITED STATES OF AMERICA

In loving memory and honor of
Grant Sneed Shockley,
Wise exemplar, Mentor,
Colleague,
Gentle friend
and
Jonathan Jackson, Jr.,
Kind friend,
Humble guide,
Wise exemplar, Model of the courage to be,
whose motto throughout his teaching vocation was
*"Christian education is that ministry which undergirds all the other
ministries of the church,"*
and who completed the final chapter in this book six months
before his death

Contents

Preface

The development of this book has been a slow and unfolding process. The process began while a group of Pan-African Christian education scholars mourned the 1996 death of Grant Sneed Shockley and celebrated his countless contributions to the lives of many during numerous years as a Christian educator, pastor, and author. Much was said about the encouragement, enlightenment, and challenge to excel that present and future leaders received from him, personally, and from reading his scholarly work. Dr. Shockley exposed the group and all of religious education to important scenes in the historical Christian education journey of black Christians, incisive critiques of the state of Christian education in the black church, and the imperative need for a liberation agenda. What came from the Pan-African group was a clear recognition of Shockley's leadership not simply as a scholar, but as a caring mentor and sage. Over time, the memory of Grant Shockley, the wise one, prompted awareness of the nagging call for wisdom in the black community. That call remains today for wise others and for black people's formation of wisdom in order for us to sojourn with integrity and hope in the twenty-first-century global village. On this basis, a cross-disciplinary and Pan-African team of writers joined together in commitment to the theme of wisdom formation and to explore specific needs for, meanings of, and educational ministry approaches to wisdom formation. Part of the process of moving forward in the project included the participation of several members of the team in a weekend forum called "Conversations on Wisdom and Wisdom Formation," which was held at Interdenominational Theological Center in Atlanta, Georgia. During that forum, we affirmed our own and others' observations that, indeed, a short supply of wisdom is prompting black people's intense search for it. We reflected on the question raised in an article by Jerry Ortiz y Pino, "What Ever Happened to Wisdom?"[1] We also queried, "Have we as a people, in fact, substituted words for wisdom that now confuse our understanding of it?" We painstakingly pondered our own views of wisdom that came from the storehouse of our experiences; and we reviewed meanings of wisdom appearing in selected resources. Our conversations brought us back to the contemporary call for intentioned focus on wisdom formation in our faith communities.

Our hope is that this volume will stimulate further conversations on wisdom and wisdom formation, and uses of the material contained here by educational leaders and other church and denominational leaders, seminarians preparing for ministry, and families within and beyond the faith community. Community leaders who work with black families and specific age/stage groups may also find this book helpful.

We wish to express our heartfelt gratitude to Dr. Reginald Crenshaw, Dr. A. Okechukwu Ogbannaya, Dr. Fred Smith, Jr., and Dr. N. Lynne Westfield who, as members of the Pan-African Scholars in Religious Education (PASRE), gave important direction in the early stages of the book's development. We are grateful as well to the Rev. Carolyn Strickland, administrative assistant in the Office of the Vice President and Academic Dean of Interdenominational Theological Center, who helped arrange location and space for the forum, "Conversations on Wisdom and Wisdom Formation." In addition, we are indebted to Mrs. Cecelia Dixon and Ms. Reta Bigham for expertly transcribing the forum tapes and processing the early manuscript copy.

Finally, it is important for us to acknowledge and express enormous appreciation to numerous unnamed individuals, church groups, seminary classes across the United States, and church leaders and laity in the global context, especially those from Britain, Zimbabwe, Ethiopia, and Bermuda. Their insights and critiques drawn from their personal lives, community experiences, and involvement in Christian educational activities contributed immensely to the direction of the writing process. They also sharpened the writers' awareness of the importance of wisdom formation and inspired the completion of the book.

—Anne E. Streaty Wimberly and Evelyn L. Parker

INTRODUCTION

In Search of Wisdom:
Necessity and Challenge

Anne E. Streaty Wimberly and Evelyn L. Parker

Only the feet of the voyager know the path.
—African proverb

The wisdom of contemporary black sages in family, church, and community, and wisdom from the African and African Diasporan heritage are becoming available increasingly in published materials.[1] These written accounts of cultural wisdom chronicle black people's personal testimonies about treacherous journeys of survival, and the attitudes, values, and profound insights about life's journey that made possible their surviving and thriving. Indeed, historically, wisdom guides and sayings from these accounts have been an integral part of the daily lives of black Christians. Over the years, these Christians have echoed and passed on to new generations phrases such as "God didn't bring us this far to leave us," "Keep on keepin' on," "There is a balm in Gilead," "Hold to God's unchanging hand," and "Don't forget where you came from." Typically, shared wisdom has taken the form of these and other oral proverbial sayings and song lines. Revered Bible verses, life stories, and commentaries on life also add to the storehouse of wisdom from which black people have drawn inspiration and guidance.

Oral wisdom from black Christian adults and forbears have been and continue to be gifts to the community precisely because of the timeless truths in them about life's realities, spiritual values, and direction for living with hope and integrity. The appearance of these materials coincides with intense interest in the black community for guidance on how to live in want and in plenty, how to surmount the storms of life, and how to face an unknown future. The sentiment among black people abounds that the current fast-paced, knowledge-rich, technological age has not satisfied deep hungers for wholeness or positive relatedness to God, self, others, and the environment.

One commentator suggests that our prevailing life circumstances are troubling in many respects, and, "in these troubled times, wisdom often seems in short supply."[2] Charles Johnston describes a more pervasive situation that demands wise response: "With growing frequency, we use the word *crisis* when defining our times. We have an environmental crisis, a drug crisis, a crisis in education, crises in love and the family."[3] And these crises touch persons with ample opportunity and abundance as well as those with insufficient benefit systems. Some writers also point to evidence in black communities of a nihilistic orientation revealed in a sense of lovelessness, hopelessness, and purposelessness stemming from continuing fractures of life in an era of depleted humanitarian concern.[4]

In the midst of life's ambiguities—trials on one hand and triumphs on the other—the fervent quest of black Christians is for wisdom necessary for choosing and acting in ways that produce wholeness. Wisdom is like what Stephen Carter calls "the serenity of a person who is confident in the knowledge that he or she is living rightly."[5] We seek wisdom that reflects an essential integrity and courage to continue on life's journey toward what is good and true with unyielding faith in God.[6] But how do we form this wisdom? What is the responsibility of black churches in guiding black people's wisdom formation?

The Nature of Christian Wisdom Formation

Christian wisdom formation refers to our ongoing journey of imagining, gaining insights, and deciding how to live as faithful and responsible Christians. As a life journey, wisdom formation relies on our recognizing that each moment opens before us anew and presents us with opportunities to see, feel, discover, and allow the life of Jesus Christ to be constantly born anew within us.[7] History has shown, though, that our path as black people can be stony and bitter; however, wisdom formation is our gaining a perspective of life that allows us to continue on. We form wisdom as we come to honest awareness that there are some dilemmas in life for which no easy resolution will come. Wisdom forms in our discovery that there are some questions for which no answer may be given, except continue on in faith by holding on to the hand of God who knows "all about our troubles, . . . will hear our faintest cry, . . . [and will] answer by and by."[8]

Christian wisdom formation has its source in God. It relies on our faith in God, openness to God, discernment of God's desire for our lives, and a commitment or sense of duty to sojourn toward the good and true that comes from our engagement in personal and corporate spiritual disciplines.[9] Among these disciplines are individual and group Scripture studying; praying; meditating; journaling; participating in retreats and worship services; probing conversations with spiritual guides and partners; listening to, responding to, and creating music; and fasting.[10] Through involvement in spiritual disciplines, we enter into a process of developing a spirituality of wisdom. In that process we move forward and reflect on a journey that is patterned after the wisdom of God that is revealed in the life and teachings of Jesus Christ proclaimed in Scriptures. And, on the wisdom-forming journey, our task is to develop the certainty of our identity as valued creations of God, our heightening appreciation of the gift of life given by God, and our deepening reverence for our own and others' lives.

Still further, Christian wisdom formation is a human relational and contextual sojourn. For Christian wisdom to be formed, past and present Christian faith exemplars must guide it. Leaders and mentors in church and community must enrich it. Our families and the entire intergenerational community must participate in it. Christian wisdom formation proceeds through the undertaking of a whole "village" in which village members commit to really be and relate with one another.

Christian wisdom formation is also a sojourn that builds on our life experiences. This nature of wisdom formation derives from our openness to and engagement in life itself, with all its promise along with its trials and tribulations. To the extent that we are ready to gain wisdom, life's experiences will offer it for us to "catch" in the form of what some call "mother wit," or our intuitive "knowing."

There is no wisdom formation without reflection. Wisdom formation requires intentional self-reflection into which the church's educational ministry must invite the wisdom seeker. Through reflection we consider the veracity of our everyday decisions and ponder whether we are acting on wisdom that comes from God's hope in us and our hope in God as well as from our imagining a way forward with God. An important aspect of Christian wisdom formation, then, is our ongoing praxis—our practice of and reflection on wise Christian living.

Stories of Wisdom Formation, God's Revelation, and the Counsel of Others

In the book *Hope and Dignity*, an old black singer named Eva Hill Roundtree tells about her journey through life and how she developed a perspective on life that enabled her to live with hope. She prefaces her testimony by saying: "I've had so many ups and downs, . . . and I've had so many burdens to carry."[11] She goes on to say that even in old age "Jesus is near you."[12] She continues:

> Without God, honey, we don't get too far. I'm not begging the Lord for nothing. I'm thanking Him for what He has done. You talk to the Lord and wait for the answer. And when you get to thinking about what the *Lord* can do, then you'll sing these songs. . . . You might get disturbed, you know. I just got disturbed last week, and I walked the length of this house and I said, "I don't let nothing separate me from the love of God."[13]

She later says that God had given her the gift of singing and that she has "helped the Lord to make me what I am."[14] Her intent was to serve the Lord by serving others, principally by singing, with the understanding that even in the smallest of churches without promise of pay, "God will expand your love" and "will pay us, if we're doing it from the heart."[15]

Eva Hill Roundtree saw God as the Source of her very being and as the Communicator of wisdom she needed for daily life. But she also regarded herself as a custodian of wisdom that comes from God and as a responsible emissary of God who not only acts wisely in the affairs of life but also continues to seek God's counsel through an ongoing relationship with God.

A middle-aged woman recalled childhood stories and incidents in her youth in which she received values, advice, discipline, and encouragement from her parents and from the congregation in which she grew up. Over time she discovered remarkable truths in what had been said to her. She admitted that, over passing years, her own approach to life has been hewn in great measure by others' wise counsel. She said that because of the wisdom she still needs, she continues to draw on the wisdom of "those who had already gained it from others and from life." She also finds herself passing on wisdom she has gained to her own children and others in her church. But she says, "We're in a brand new day of the Web, information oversaturation, HIV/AIDS, violence, family conflicts and breakups, you name it. So, there are special needs calling for extraordinary wisdom."

These brief stories offer us personalized ways of seeing and entering into an exploration of the nature of wisdom formation. Both stories convey to us an understanding that wisdom formation moves forth with the development of positive insights and understandings of who and whose we are. Wisdom formation is recognizable in our ability to cope with life's complexities, make sensible judgments, and exhibit responsible behavior. The Christian orientation to wisdom formation also includes our coming to know the qualities of God exhibited in Jesus Christ, our seeking after those qualities, and our making those qualities and the spiritual values undergirding them part of our everyday sojourn in community.

Facing Challenges to Wisdom Formation in an Information Age

In the earlier mentioned story, one woman pointed out that today there are "special needs calling for extraordinary wisdom." Her statement highlights a difficulty in forming wisdom today. The situation is compounded in this age of "information oversaturation" by our propensity to falsely equate wisdom with bare knowledge.

Mortimer Adler describes knowledge as organized information or information that is put together in some systematic way.[16] However systematic it may be, knowledge needs to be *"understood* knowledge, not just *bare* knowledge."[17] *Understood* knowledge refers to a kind of knowing that gives direction to the conduct of our lives and our societies on the basis of a coherent set of values. Adler describes this kind of knowledge as "prescriptive" or "obligatory" knowing.[18] Within this knowing lies our vision of an obligatory and wholeness-producing goal in life for self and community as well as the means of making this goal a reality. Prescriptive knowing goes beyond what Adler calls "descriptive" or "explanatory" knowing, which is our knowing something as a fact, including what something is and why it is.[19] For Christians, *understood* knowledge has to do with our appropriation, though finite, of who Jesus Christ is, the nature of life and ministry he modeled, and what this knowing means for our defining and developing ourselves as fuller and more faithful selves in Christ. It is the kind of knowing that reflects our awareness of our reason for being—our knowing that our lives are to be lived after Jesus' example. It is awareness that impels us to struggle with the choices placed before us in a world of seemingly infinite options and to "put ourselves on the line" to choose what points toward wholeness for ourselves and our communities.[20]

It is also important to add that knowledge is also "perspectival." Knowledge has to do with our imagining, not simply our reason for being, but our perceiving, appreciating, and relating to the One in whom we anchor our lives. "Perspectival" knowledge also allows freedom to doubt, question, lament life's realities, and to unlearn and relearn meanings of faith throughout life, to paraphrase J. Glenn Gray's words.[21]

Understanding develops to the extent that we become tied up in ongoing creative reflections on our life's goals and perspectives and on meanings of communal wholeness. This kind of understanding leads to wisdom. It is generally understood, too, that wisdom forms through our actual experiences of life, and the practical knowledge that accrues from these experiences. Life can be a powerful teacher.

Wisdom Formation in Lifelong Perspective

The women's stories mentioned earlier remind us that wisdom formation is lifelong and intentional. We form it over time through information and values received from others, remembering what we receive, discerning the salience of what we receive, and deciding whether or how best to act on it. The lifelong nature of wisdom formation suggests, too, that movement into our adult and older adult years does not automatically imbue us with wisdom. While wisdom formation can be cumulative, each life age/stage calls for new insights to address newly emerging circumstances. We also know that there are persons who continue toward and into older adulthood with negative attitudes, destructive behavior, and seemingly without any sense of purpose or meaning. Conversely, it is not entirely uncommon to know or meet individuals in younger generations who in their daily living articulate and carry out a profound understanding of the nature of life and their role in it. Whatever the case, wisdom formation most often requires guidance and support, an individual's openness to it, and readiness to embrace it. And our churches have an important responsibility in helping this process to unfold.

Wisdom Formation as Gift Sharing in Black Churches

Appearing over and over in what we have already shared is the notion that wisdom is not a commodity achieved and held in isolation by the Christian sojourner. Wisdom is a God-given, communally guided and shared quality of our coming to know, understand, appreciate, and act on what it means to sojourn as Christians amidst life's ambiguities. Becoming wise in these ways is furthered through the sharing of gifts of insight in the company of others in the "village." Our churches are essential faith "villages" that generate this wisdom formation through giving gifts of time, information, insights, encouragement, and praise.[22] Let us illustrate through stories and then invite you, the reader, into reflection on the gift of wisdom given to you by others.

Anne's and Evelyn's Stories

In writing this introduction, we too have reflected on and shared with each other our own stories of the black church's support of our development of wisdom. For example, Anne remembered a time in her own early adult life, after the loss of their fourth child due to difficulty in carrying babies to full term, she became overcome with grief. She found it difficult to see life in any positive way. At a church meeting, while she was in the midst of that trying time, the oldest member of the church came to Anne, put her arms around her, and whispered, "Nothing can separate us from the love of God." This woman whom everyone knew as "Mom Parker" continued by telling Anne that she had noticed Anne's downward demeanor. Mom Parker said that she could not know exactly all Anne was feeling since she was not "in Anne's shoes," but that she knew something of Anne's pain because of her own inability to have children. Anne asked her, "Why did God single my husband and me out for this terrible loss?" Mom Parker simply replied, "There is no easy answer, but I know that God did not forsake me, and God has not forsaken you. God does have a plan for your life. You can be sure of that!"

Mom Parker continued, "It's like the old folks before me used to sing: 'Sometimes I feel discouraged and think my works in vain; but then the Holy Spirit revives my soul again. There is a balm in Gilead to make the wounded whole.' Don't forget, too, that I'm here for you." Mom Parker continued to hold Anne tightly. She then told Anne of the help she had seen Anne give to others, and of the gifts God had given Anne that she had already shared and would continue to share even though Anne might not now believe it. Mom Parker reminded Anne of the beauty of womanhood that the loss of children would not take away. She concluded by saying, "I know the road ahead may not be easy, but strength will come if you believe in your heart that 'Nothing can separate you from the love of God,' and that 'God will make a way somehow.' "

Anne has never forgotten this sage's gift of wisdom. Mom Parker was a "teacher" who shared a perspective on life that eluded Anne at that juncture in Anne's sojourn. Because of Mom Parker's time, insights, encouragement, and praise, Anne became wiser and felt empowered to go on with life.

Evelyn remembers the wisdom of Mrs. Daisy Cole, a retired teacher and district director of Christian education in the Christian Methodist Episcopal Church. Mrs. Cole mentored Evelyn during Evelyn's young adult years and was God's instrument for solidifying her call to professional educational ministry. Although Mrs. Cole suffered from glaucoma, she never allowed her illness to hinder her service to the educational ministry of the church. She especially enjoyed teaching adult Sunday school classes, where she always developed graphs and charts to illustrate her presentation. She was a symbol of wisdom because she embodied perseverance and hope. Through the years her frail physical condition made it difficult to read, walk, cook, and clean her home. However, she never stopped reading, writing, and developing graphs and charts that illustrated her solid biblical interpretations of the Sunday school lesson. She consistently refused to be helped in walking up and down the steep steps of the church but learned to negotiate the steps using the handrail.

Mrs. Cole was approachable for conversation and counsel, always pointing toward the possibilities in the midst of problems. Her inviting spirit assuaged the potential intimidation that a twenty-year-old might feel in the presence of an eighty-year-old symbol of fortitude. After politically negotiating Evelyn as her successor as district director of Christian education, Mrs. Cole announced her retirement. During her retirement years, she continued to be available to respond to Evelyn's questions and concerns. She was Evelyn's wise guide, always pointing her to hope.

The Necessity of Shared Gifts in Black Churches

The stories we shared highlight the importance of the Christian faith community in which the wise share gifts that can result in the wisdom formation of others. While it is possible that this kind of shared wisdom happens more on an informal basis and without explicit attention from the congregational and educational leadership levels, the perplexities of our day really do demand more intentionality in promoting and developing a context of sharing. In order for this to happen, our faith communities must come to awareness that, for all of us—children, youth, and adults alike—ongoing wisdom formation depends greatly on gifts of time created to be with one another, time created to hear and respond to one another's stories of both challenging and positive situations, or to simply be the non-anxious caring presence.

There are specific needs for the various ages/stages too. The wisdom formation of our young requires exemplars who embody wisdom in the way they live their lives as well as who can tell the stories of how they have "come this far by faith" over the rough places along life's journey. Likewise, these exemplars must be willing to hear the stories of the young in order to become aware of the distinctive issues they face. The important role of the listener is to attend to the struggles of and the blocks against acting wisely that youth confront.

As we advance in age, the spiritual partner or advisor is needed to share stories of trial and triumph, to advise, and to give encouragement when we are less than confident about ourselves, others, and even God in our daily journey. Across every age/stage, the predictable crises of life, personal and communal issues, and experiences associated with blackness require affirming interactions and discourse that can help us sustain and act with a hope-filled perspective. The black church is called to respond to these realities through educational ministry that fosters the sharing of gifts of wisdom. These gifts open the way for moments of discernment about the circumstances of our lives, and a time of decision on how we will, in fact, continue our life's journey.

To the extent that black churches make possible these wisdom-forming and wisdom-sustaining initiatives, they enliven educational ministry. Indeed, to the extent that black churches acknowledge the necessity of offering and exchanging gifts of wisdom on behalf of black people's ongoing wisdom formation, these faith communities act on a critical twenty-first-century requirement for educational ministry. This kind of acknowledgment by black churches is, of course, only the first step toward accepting wisdom-directed responsibility that entails taking time to listen, share stories and insights, give encouragement, and make certain of the ongoing presence of affirming interactions and discourse. Steps are also needed to identify and implement concrete models and approaches for forming wisdom needed by black children, youth, and adults to face these days. This book seeks to provide these steps.

The Invitation to Read Further

In the following chapters, readers are invited to explore ways of engaging in wisdom-forming educational ministries. The chapters present specific models and approaches that have been used by the authors to contribute to the wisdom formation of black persons in a variety of contexts and in the various ages/stages. The reader will find a unique blend of ideas from scholars in Hebrew Bible, Christian education, and pastoral care and psychology, and links that were forged between the academy and the faith community. We now invite you, the reader, to join in the search for wisdom, to discover new or renewed insights on wisdom, and to envision ways you may contribute to others' wisdom formation.

CHAPTER 1

Forming Wisdom:
Biblical and African Guides

Temba L. J. Mafico

Does not wisdom call,
    and does not understanding raise her voice?
On the heights, beside the way,
    at the crossroads she takes her stand;
beside the gates in front of the town,
    at the entrance of the portals she cries out:
"To you, O people, I call, and my cry is to all that live."
                                        —*Proverbs 8:1-4*

There is much that challenges us in our third millennium world. Struggles abound in our families, in and across our churches and denominations, within and between class and cultural groups, and in the wider global community. There is a hunger among us for answers to the trials and tribulations of life, and to questions about hope in the midst of oppression and even under the threat of untimely death. The quest in our communities is also for responses to deep wonderment about the activity of God in the midst of life's realities. The concerns resound: Where may wisdom be found to address the challenges of our day? How may we act wisely along the journey of life we are set upon? What do we say to our young to inspire their wisdom formation?

The queries of our communities today parallel those raised in traditional Israelite and African culture. And there is much from both traditions that can enliven the discussion on wisdom and the formation of wisdom of Africans and Africans in the Diaspora. In this opening chapter, we will explore the Israelite and African conceptualization of wisdom by giving several examples from the Israelite and African religiocultural lives. The Israelite perspective will be based primarily on Wisdom Literature of the Hebrew Bible/Old Testament. The African perspective will be based on the general African practice of eldership and its relationship to wisdom. The chapter will end with a summary of the striking similarities that exist between the Israelite and African concept of wisdom and knowledge.

Israelite Concepts of Wisdom and Wisdom Formation

Four books of the Bible present the essence of the Israelite concept of wisdom: Proverbs, Ecclesiastes, Job, and the apocryphal book of Sirach. The wisdom that these books present is most particularly a practical capacity for coping with life, and the pursuit of a principled life. Moreover, wisdom's source is God.[1] The wisdom found in these books contrasts with the strong emphasis on knowledge that often pervades current-day conceptions of wisdom. Indeed, Lawrence O. Richards makes the pointed statement that "the scriptures do not make the mistake of confusing wisdom with other mental capacities or of giving wisdom less than its central place."[2] The role of the sage is important. According to Hebrew tradition, the sage's purpose is to communicate the messages of wisdom gleaned from experience in order that the receivers will gain insights for coping with life.

The most striking aspect of wisdom in the ancient Middle East is its universalism. It is for this reason that biblical Wisdom Literature is devoid of important biblical concepts such as covenant, commandments, the Exodus, or even the patriarchs. Wisdom, as Roland E. Murphy noticed, "is an international heritage in which Israel had a share."[3] The book of Proverbs regards wisdom as God's greatest attribute. It is by wisdom that God created the world (Proverbs 3:19). The equation of wisdom and God led the Israelites to affirm that "the fear of the LORD is the beginning of [wisdom]" (Proverbs 1:7). Proverbs indicates further that the person who finds wisdom and has understanding is very blessed and happy (Proverbs 3:13-14). Indeed, wisdom is not simply identified as a person, but as one with feminine qualities.

Wisdom, like the earth, is portrayed as a woman who is desired because, like the earth, wisdom sustains life. This feminine quality of sustenance or of being the lifeline for human existence is pivotal to views on both understanding and wisdom. Thus, understanding (Heb., *binah*) and wisdom (Heb., *hokmah*), are feminine.

Promotion of Wisdom Formation in the Young

An important emphasis in Israelite culture regards the teaching of wisdom to the young. The book of Proverbs is replete with short stories, proverbs, observations, and the elder's instructions given to the youth through pithy statements. In Proverbs 4:1-9, for example, we read of a father's instructions to his child. Instead of telling the child to sit and listen to orders, the father asked the child to listen to a story pertaining to the father's childhood and what his own father said to him:

> When I was a son with my father,
>   tender, and my mother's favorite,
> he taught me, and said to me,
> "Let your heart hold fast my words;
> Keep my commandments, and live.
> Get wisdom; get insight: do not forget, nor turn away
> from the words of my mouth.
> Do not forsake her, and she will keep you;
> love her, and she will guard you.
> The beginning of wisdom is this: Get wisdom,
> and whatever else you get, get insight.
> Prize her highly, and she will exalt you;
> she will honor you if you embrace her.
> She will place on your head a fair garland;
> she will bestow on you a beautiful crown."
>   (Proverbs 4:3-9)

This didactic discourse story is very revealing of the Israelite transmission of wisdom to children. By this short biographical sketch, the parent enabled the child to learn wisdom through a powerfully engaging dual narrative approach: storytelling/story-listening and visualization. The storytelling enabled the children to hear the story of their parent's past and to construct a "picture" wherein they could "see" that their parents were also once children of their own parents. The storytelling/story-listening and visualization were channels for the children's wisdom formation.

There are texts in Proverbs that explicitly emphasize that children should observe natural phenomena in order to form wisdom. For example, in Proverbs 6:6-9 we read:

> Go to the ant, you lazybones;
> consider [her] ways, and be wise.
> Without having any chief or officer or ruler,
> [she] prepares [her] food in summer,
> and gathers [her] sustenance in harvest.
> How long will you lie there, O lazybones?
> When will you rise from your sleep?[4]

As in the biographical sketch appearing in Proverbs 4:3-9, the method for bringing about the children's wisdom formation was that of storytelling/story-listening and visualization. There is one addition, however. The question that appears in verse 9 is a logical corollary to the verses that precede it. Verse 9 actually presents both challenge and motivation to observe the ant. In this case, the expectation was for the children to act on their visualization of the narrative that was being shared with them. The insertion of this verse suggests that lecturing *about* the ant or simply *telling* the story *about* the ant's ways was not sufficient to engender the children's wisdom formation. Wisdom formation requires an actual experience with which the children can identify and from which they can gain critical insights. Consequently, the story in which an ant is the central character reflects the context and time when the requirements for success were in terms of agricultural skills, hunting, and raising livestock—logical settings for viewing the ways of an ant. More important, the story of the ant was followed by words to underscore not simply the primacy of the wisdom gained by observing the ant, but the consequences of failing to do so as indicated in the following:

> A little sleep, a little slumber,
> a little folding of the hands to rest,
> and poverty will come upon you like a robber,
> and want, like an armed warrior. (Proverbs 6:10-11)

The parent reinforces the wisdom-directed pedagogy by telling two more short stories. These stories extend beyond the contrasting theme of consequences of failing to seek wisdom (vv. 10-11). Emphasis lies on the villainous character and calamitous fate of persons who are void of wisdom (vv. 12-15), and character flaws that God hates as well as that become an abomination (vv. 16-19). The abhorrent character traits include haughty eyes, a lying tongue, murder, evil heart, false testimony, and propensity to foster discord.

The Primacy of Experience in Wisdom Formation

Earlier attention was given to the parental storyteller's expectation that the young story-listeners will actually experience that which they hear and visualize. This emphasis in Hebrew biblical literature is a pivotal pedagogical approach in wisdom formation endeavors. Consequently, it is important to give additional attention to it.

With regard to historical events, wisdom was acquired not so much by listening to the accounts, but by reenacting the events themselves. By so doing, persons at any age reenact the events in ritual performances that are intended to reactivate the potency of wisdom. This emphasis of the Israelites derived from their view of history as a series of experiences through which indispensable insights could form in people. Although our primary focus here is on the four books of the Bible that best disclose the Israelite concept of wisdom and wisdom formation, it is instructive that the book of Genesis does not give lessons *about* God or other theological concepts. The book simply relates some stories about the patriarchs and their families. In a communal-oriented society, persons removed as far as the fourth generation were not to regard themselves as separate from their progenitors. What the ancestors experienced, they too experience, if not vicariously, then ritually. The reader is expected to visualize the events of the patriarchs and to acquire wisdom by reciting in a sanctuary their situations and circumstances. One example of this is found in Deuteronomy 26:5b-10a:

> "A wandering Aramean was my ancestor; he went down into
> Egypt and lived there as an alien, few in number, and there he

became a great nation, mighty and populous. When the Egyptians treated us harshly and afflicted us, by imposing hard labor on us, we cried to the LORD, the God of our ancestors; the LORD heard our voice and saw our affliction, our toil, and our oppression. The LORD brought us out of Egypt with a mighty hand and an outstretched arm, with a terrifying display of power, and with signs and wonders; and he brought us into this place and gave us this land, a land flowing with milk and honey. So now I bring the first of the fruit of the ground that you, O LORD, have given me."

Scholars attribute the book of Deuteronomy to the period between the mid-seventh and sixth century B.C.E.[5] This period was a lengthy time after the Exodus. Gerhard von Rad believes that the text presented above is the first creed that was recited by people of later generations in order to tie them covenantally with the people of the Exodus, in this case Jacob.[6] But we should notice that the worshiper is made to identify, in a dramatic way, with the ancestors who experienced the Exodus. First, he or she must affirm that the first patriarch, who in this case is most likely Jacob, was his or her real father.[7] Following this acknowledgment, the worshiper must recite the parent's experiences in the land and the sojourn to Egypt. Up to this point, the worshiper is relating the story that has been heard. But in verse 6, he or she must identify with the most painful portion of the history by reciting the slavery and oppression in Egypt as a personal experience in the following way:

> The Egyptians treated *us* harshly and afflicted *us*, by imposing hard labor on *us, we* cried to the LORD, the God of *our* ancestors; the LORD heard *our* voice and saw *our* affliction, *our* toil, and *our* oppression. The LORD brought *us* out of Egypt with a mighty hand and an outstretched arm, with a terrifying display of power, and with signs and wonders; and he brought *us* into this place and gave *us* this land. (Deuteronomy 26:6-9*a*; italics added)

The reciter is no longer a spectator or observer of a historical episode that took place so many years before his or her time; rather, the reciter sees himself or herself as a participant in a contemporary episode in which God is active. By identifying with one's historical past, the reciter becomes more historically rooted and concludes, "So now I bring the first of the fruit of the ground that you, O LORD, have given me." The creed shifts from the retelling of history to the reciter's participation into that history, which can lead to self-realization and identity, a centerpiece in the formation of wisdom.

The Wisdom Literature does not provide an unvarying account of the results of the search for wisdom derived from experience. The book of Ecclesiastes more than Proverbs is replete with stories and observations that disclose the distinctive pessimistic world-view of Qoheleth, the disputed acronym for Ecclesiastes or the one whom some Bible commentators regard as an assembly speaker.[8] The stories and observations of Qoheleth show evidence of a search for wisdom; but the results of Qoheleth's reflections on life's journey convey a stark denial of wisdom's power to provide a sure anchor for one's existence.[9] Because of the monotonous circularity of life, Qoheleth concludes that life is boring because there is nothing new under the sun (Ecclesiastes 1:9). Qoheleth questions the value of drawing on insights from past experiences since choices confound one's knowing the road yet to be taken (Ecclesiastes 4:4-6). Life's experiences of dissatisfaction, disappointment, wisdom's mysteries, overlooked wisdom, risk, predictability, and futility that unfold over the chapters of the book result in the conclusion that whatever human beings do under the sun is vanity, like chasing after the wind.[10] What appears in the book has the effect of highlighting blocks along the journey of life with which the reader/listener may identify. And what is noteworthy in this Israelite Wisdom Literature is that the elder, presumably Solomon now in his old age, grants to the reader/listener what some call a "painful education" or wisdom through his reflection on his observations and experiences of life.[11]

The Distinctive Wisdom of the Book of Job

An earlier reference pointed to Qoheleth's observations and experiences that provide a "painful education" or wisdom through focusing on life's unpleasant realities. In the book of Job, a similar plot unfolds, though in this case God heaps disaster on Job, who seemingly has done nothing to deserve it. However, in contrast to Qoheleth's stark denial of wisdom's power to provide a sure anchor for one's existence, Job enters into fervent lament and conversation with God; and even in the midst of his torment he declares,

> For I know that my Redeemer lives,
> and that at the last he will stand upon the earth;
> and after my skin has been thus destroyed,
> then in my flesh I shall see God,
> whom I shall see on my side,
> and my eyes shall behold, and not another. (Job 19:25-27)

This declaration of Job also highlights the kind of wisdom formation identified in the introduction of this book. This wisdom is reflected in one's coming to honest personal awareness that there are some questions in the midst of the hard trials of life for which no answer will suffice, except "Continue in faith."

There is an additional aspect of the book of Job that merits mention here, and that feature regards the connection between wisdom and age. In Job 32:4-6 Elihu, a young man, had not talked during the earlier discourses. He was waiting for his turn after the elders had stopped talking. It is for this reason that the text reads:

> Now Elihu had waited to speak to Job, because they were older than he. But when Elihu saw that there was no answer in the mouths of these three men, he became angry. Elihu son of Barachel the Buzite answered:
>
> "I am young in years,
> and you are aged;
> therefore I was timid and afraid
> to declare my opinion to you.
> I said, 'Let days speak,
> and many years teach wisdom.' "

Elihu's silence before the elders is also typical of Africans, as seen below in the opening story on African wisdom.

African Concepts of Wisdom and Wisdom Formation

It is accepted in the African context that the role of the elder is important. As in the Hebrew tradition, the elder is regarded as a sage and is given responsibility to communicate the wisdom gleaned from experience for the benefit of the young's wisdom formation. I am aware of the following story of a young man named Fungai, who is rebuked by an elder for presuming that he could enlighten the elders with his scholarly analysis of political facts:

> There was a young man in Zimbabwe called Fungai. He was a brilliant young man who earned a college degree in political science with honors. After completing his college studies, he was appointed to the post of principal at a school in the village where villagers held high respect for their elders. Fungai commanded great respect as a fine administrator. One day he entered a conversation with some villagers who had little to no elementary education. When the discussion turned to political problems facing the country, Fungai was appalled by their illogical analysis of the facts. Without seeking permission to speak, he confronted one of the old men with the retort, "Let me tell you . . ." The senior elder shouted at him saying, "Young man, look at my gray hair and beard. Look at my wrinkled face. I have seen many things. What have you seen which you can tell us? When you are among elders, keep quiet and learn wisdom!"

In current Western societies where intentioned cross-generational relationships are limited, the question may be raised about the denial of the young man's contribution to the conversation. There is, to be sure, an expressed concern among the young that their voices are silenced, that their concerns go unheeded; and because they are not listened to, they feel set adrift on the raging sea of life. At the same time, adults do not always feel respected by the young and, in their busyness, they are often guilty of avoiding contact with the young. Moreover, as stated in the introduction, age alone does not necessarily assure wisdom. In Fungai's case, the problem was not that the elders did not want to accept his input. The concern was for his assumption that he had the final word on the issue based on his erudition. This ran contrary to the cultural value of people taking their turns in a discussion beginning with the most elderly and moving down to the youngest, or vice versa.[12]

The situation with Fungai draws attention to the disrespect

shown the elderly men, and Fungai's presumption of the heightened value of book knowledge over experience. The elderly man's response was as if to say,

> There is nothing new under the sun.
> Is there a thing of which it is said,
>   "See, this is new"?
> It has already been,
> in the ages before us." (Ecclesiastes 1:9c-10)

Again, Fungai's story is not about the young's being forbidden to participate in cross-generational conversation. Nor is it meant to deny the problematic lifestyles of some elderly adults that call their wisdom into question. Rather, the point here is that, like the Israelite Wisdom Literature, the story from the African context contributes to the awareness of third-millennium Africans and Africans in the Diaspora regarding the importance of the elderly's role in sharing wisdom hewn by experience. It highlights the big difference between knowledge and wisdom in traditional African culture. Africans, like Israelites, believe that a person might have much education but still lack wisdom. Conversely, a person may not have a formal education and yet be full of wisdom.

It is important to recognize, too, that African wisdom, although not written down like that of the Israelites and other people of the ancient Middle East, was in many ways similar. An elder passed wisdom on to the young by telling stories and proverbs, teaching songs, and relating tales with a clearly articulated or imbedded moral meaning. One story my mother taught to me and other children when I was young is about a man who was experiencing abject poverty. The man always wished he were rich like other people he observed as being wealthy. The story is as follows:

> One day, the man met a deer who asked him why he was so lugubrious. The man related to the deer his ordeals with poverty. The deer was very sympathetic toward the man. The deer gave him a pumpkin seed and advised him to grow and water it every day. The deer also told the man that when the seed bore pumpkins, he should pick the pumpkins, feed his family, and keep the seeds in a basket. Thereafter, every morning he should do three things. First, he must check on

how the deer is doing. Second, he must go to check on how the pumpkin plant is doing and pick some more pumpkins. Last, he should check on the seeds in the basket. This was all that was required for him to do to be rich.

The man was thrilled that he could, at long last, feed his family. On the first day he went to check on the deer. The deer told of feeling all right although aged and feeble. Next, the man went to the pumpkin plant and found it growing luxuriously with flowers and promising to bear many pumpkins. He repeated this process every morning, including checking on the basket. To his amazement, every morning when he checked on the basket, it had gold coins. But before he counted them, he went to check on the rapidly aging and frail deer.

However, as the gold coins increased, so did his preoccupation with counting and banking the money. He then delegated the responsibility of checking on the deer to his son; and he asked his son to report back to him. At first, the son did as his father had told him. Later, however, he too became busy playing games he purchased with the gold coins, and so he did not check on the deer, nor did the father ask for a report.

Finally, the deer died and the man did not know about it. He realized that something was wrong because the pumpkin plant was withering and bearing no pumpkins. The gold coins were reverting to seeds again. He decided to go and check on the deer and to tell the deer about the vicissitudes of his situation. He was shocked to discover that the deer had been dead for many days. By being derelict of the simple duty of checking on the deer, poverty returned.

Although Mother did not directly apply the story to us, we got its intended message that we should not tire of expressing our gratitude to those who bless our lives. As I grew up, the story remained alive in my mind and kept on exuding wisdom on me. I began to realize that the deer was my aging parents who will become increasingly dependent on me for their sustenance.

There is another village story, told by my father in Zimbabwe, that had a decided effect on my own wisdom formation.

A hunter could not bring home a kill because he always listened to a bird's advice.[13] Other hunters were bringing home rabbits and several small animals, thus making their families happy. But this one hunter was bringing no animal home for food. Whenever he aimed at a small animal, the bird in a tree said in the Shona language, *Rekezvo, zviuya zvirimberiyo"* (Do not shoot, because the best is yet to come). This advice was repeated many times, and he heeded it. After a long time had passed, the man went to hunt and saw a buffalo. He aimed at it. The bird did not stop him. He struck the buffalo right through the heart; and the animal died. The whole village came to see his kill and to help him carry the meat home. A great feast was held, with much meat, singing, and dancing to herald the greatest hunter of the village.

Like Mother, Dad did not apply the story directly to us. He simply told the story. We listened, and we clearly understood the message. When I was in the seventh grade, I began to be interested in dating girls. My mother advised me to wait because better girls were waiting in the future. It was easy for me to accept this advice because of my memory of the story of the hunter and the bird, and the resulting wisdom that story imparted. The same wise message disclosed in the story had an impact on my life in other ways. In one instance, most of my classmates completed high school and sought jobs. I listened to the bird that advised me to wait because the best was yet to come, and it did.

The pedagogical approach taken by my parents was similar to the strategy appearing in the Israelite Wisdom Literature to which I referred earlier. Storytelling and story-listening functioned as narrative tools for disclosing wisdom for use in life situations. Moreover, like the Wisdom Literature, the stories of my parents made possible my visualization of the scenes portrayed in them, my identification with the activity in the scenes, and my grasping the central meaning of the story.

Besides telling stories, Africans also speak in proverbs. The one that had great influence on the young when I was growing up, and perhaps continues to exert similar appeal today, is called in the Shona language *Upfumi tange nhamo* (To be rich, begin poor). This proverb was augmented by another one: *Chidoko ndimarera muiri, chikuru chinozoza wakora* (A small morsel preserves the body. The banquet comes much later). These two proverbs, among several others, conveyed to youths a wise orientation to life which was to be satisfied with the little God gave them. At the same time, the proverbs encourage youths to continue to aspire for better things that are to come.

Africans also sought to bring about the formation of wisdom in their young through the very names they gave to their children. Indeed, one such Shona name is *Kurauwone*, a sapiental sentence name meaning "Grow up and realize (the reality of this world)." When later in life that person sees, for example, injustice, he will not become overly depressed because he has been expecting both the good and the bad as part of life.

New Testament Concepts of Wisdom and Pedagogical Approaches

Of course it is important to add here that the New Testament continues the emphasis on wisdom begun in the Israelite tradition. Jesus, as a Jewish rabbi (teacher), employed wisdom formation as a pedagogical method. Jesus taught a way of living, a basic image of reality, and an ethos and ethic. In wisdom, two alternatives to live are always presented: the wise way and the foolish way; the righteous way and the wicked way; the way of life and the way of death. Jesus employed several wisdom-focused pedagogical methods. First, he taught in parables, which were short stories that illuminated the point he was making. Jesus was inviting his hearers to see reality in a new or different way.

In addition to parables, Jesus used aphorisms, some of which were similar to parables. However, they included beatitudes, nature sayings, and proverbs. The aphorisms were well-phrased, compact, memorable, and evocative, ushering listeners into fresh insights on truth and reality. Although New Testament scholars draw a fine line between aphorisms and proverbs, proverbs and aphorisms serve the same purpose of stimulating thought and leading the hearer to look at things and a way of living in a new light. For example, the aphorisms "Figs are not gathered from thorns, nor are grapes picked from a bramble bush" (Luke 6:44; Matthew 7:16); "No one can serve two masters" (Matthew 6:24;

Luke 16:13); "If a blind man leads a blind man, both will fall into a pit" (Matthew 15:14 RSV; Luke 6:39) are identical to proverbs, albeit Jesus might have coined them. Jesus' presentation of the wise and the foolish way appear in Matthew 7:24-27 and Luke 6:47-49; and the narrow way and the broad way in Matthew 7:13-14 (see also Luke 13:23-24). Again, by this way of teaching, Jesus stimulated his audience's formation of wisdom by kindling their reexamination of life as they lived it, and their aspiration to a more wise way of living that was consistent with the reign of God.

Like the sages before him, Jesus called his hearers to observe nature and to learn from natural things. He told them to consider the birds of the air, and the lilies of the field that neither sow nor reap, nor toil nor spin, and yet God makes them more sparkling than even King Solomon in his glory (Matthew 6:26-30; Luke 12:24-28). So also the sun rises on the evil and the good, and rain falls on the just and the unjust (Matthew 5:45). Obviously, the audience was familiar with Jesus' references; and these references enabled the hearers to "peep" into the nature of God and God's reign.

The teaching of Jesus also led to a new paradigm for behavior. The conventional wisdom of his day primarily focused on personal purity or holiness. However, Jesus consistently stressed compassion. Several parables demonstrate this behavioral paradigm of wisdom: the father of the prodigal son had compassion (Luke 15:20), as did the good Samaritan (Luke 10:33). However, the unmerciful servant did not show compassion (Matthew 18:23-35). In the wisdom sayings, Jesus underscored the point that believers in God should strive toward a compassionate way of living because God in whom they believed is a compassionate God.

With the exception of Pauline literature, much of which is theological discourse, the New Testament exhibits several ways of communicating wisdom. The New Testament also stresses wisdom that is based on observations of and reflection on life experiences.

Some Concluding Comments on Biblical and African Guides to Wisdom Formation

In the African context, as in the Israelite Wisdom Literature in particular, there is no demarcation between age and experience.

However, knowledge about facts is neither regarded as sufficient nor as fully trustworthy unless those facts can be backed up by real-life experiences. The experiences of life provide an important footing for factual knowledge. Of course it is not fair to say that knowledge, intelligence, and extraordinary ability, which adults and young people may all possess, is despised. Nonetheless, the notion is conveyed in the African context and in the Israelite Wisdom Literature that to know *about* or to have some hypothesis or theories *about* a thing is not the same as experiencing it. Wisdom is reckoned as a diverse gift that tends to come with age. It is for this reason that age is accorded status in every situation. However, by basing wisdom on experience, the ancients in biblical times also realized that only God had infinite wisdom. Proverbs 21:30 declares: "No wisdom, no understanding, no counsel, can avail against the LORD."

Several proverbs refer to the ancients' realization that there were certain limit-situations in their observations and experiences. Experience brought them wisdom on the importance of planning for any venture, especially for war (Proverbs 20:18). Nevertheless, they also realized that no matter the number of horses, "victory belongs to the LORD" (Proverbs 21:31). The realm of experience, to which the sages constantly resorted, also indicated to them that certainty was not always assured. The sages of Israel experienced a mystery of being as well as certainty about particular facts. For example, Proverbs 16:1-2, 9 reads:

> The plans of the mind belong to mortals,
> but the answer of the tongue
>   is from the LORD.
> All one's ways may be pure in one's own eyes,
> but the LORD weighs the spirit. . . .
> The human mind plans the way,
> but the LORD directs the steps.

The sages also warned against the assumption that a person may possess wisdom. One should be aware that wisdom based on human experience is limited and can blind a person to reality:

> Do you see persons wise in their own eyes?
> There is more hope for fools than for them. (Proverbs 26:12)

Do not be wise in your own eyes,
fear the LORD, and turn away from evil. (Proverbs 3:7)

In Job 11:7-8, Zophar said to Job:

"Can you find out the deep things of God?
Can you find the limit of the Almighty?
It is higher than heavens—what can you do?
Deeper than the Sheol—what can you know?

In Job 36:22, 26, Elihu perhaps provides a fitting conclusion to the limitations of wisdom:

See, God is exalted in his power;
Who is a teacher like him?
Surely, God is great, and we do not know him;
the number of his years is unsearchable.

The Israelite Wisdom Literature and the Africans convey the belief that although creation and life are a mystery, there is some inalienable order that governs the universe.

Conclusion

The discussion in this chapter began with the question in Proverbs 8:1, "Does not wisdom call, and does not understanding raise her voice?" This led us to ask, "Where may wisdom be found to address the challenges of our day? How may we act wisely along the journey of life we are set upon? What do we say to our young to inspire their wisdom formation?" In response to the questions, this chapter has invited us to explore the formation of wisdom in biblical times and in African tradition. The pivotal pedagogical approach discovered in the exploration is that the formation of wisdom in both historical contexts involved listening to the elders' accounts of the vicissitudes of their lives and observing natural phenomenon. These two approaches are pivotal in our pursuit of wisdom. While book knowledge is important and necessary, it is the experiences of real life, both favorable and challenging, and reflection on those experiences, that are exceedingly helpful in our formation of wisdom.

The importance of the contributions of life experiences to wisdom formation is found in the lessons taught particularly by the books of Proverbs, Job, and Ecclesiastes. These writings point out that real wisdom is based on experiences more so than on intellect that is sharpened through book knowledge. Apart from experience, our reflections on life and our discernment of "what's next" on life's journey should be placed within the context of our relationship with God, trust in God, and on our consciousness of God's wisdom and the meaning of living according to God's reign and righteousness. Thus, wisdom formation in biblical and African tradition is based on the premise, "The fear [reverence] of the LORD is the beginning of wisdom" (Proverbs 1:7a). This view of divine wisdom makes possible our continuing on the sojourn of life even in the midst of the very hardships for which we blame God. Indeed, we are enabled to contemplate the way forward only through reliance on God's wisdom that is accessed through a continuing relationship with God. Like Job, a wise person experiencing inexplicable anguish is enabled to say, "Though he slay me, yet will I trust in him" (Job 13:15a KJV); and, "Naked I came from my mother's womb, and naked shall I return there; the LORD gave, and the LORD has taken away; blessed be the name of the LORD" (Job 1:21). True wisdom is divine wisdom. The process of its formation is to seek first the reign of God and God's righteousness (Matthew 6:33). Thereafter, everything else makes sense.

CHAPTER 2

Forming Wisdom Through Cultural Rootedness

Yolanda Y. Smith

To go back to tradition is the first step forward.
—African proverb[1]

Wisdom formation must become a central and intentional focus of educational ministry in black churches in order to assure black personhood, hope, and liberative action in the third millennium. Educational ministry of this sort guides black people's formation of insights, values, and ways of being and acting as self-assured Christians by bringing about their critical consciousness of wisdom inherent in the black cultural heritage. An experience of mine highlights the need for attention to a cultural rootedness approach to wisdom formation.

Several years ago, I had the privilege of visiting a Christian school in Los Angeles on a field trip assignment for my contemporary theories in religious education class. Each class enrollee was required to visit a religious education program that reflected a particular cultural perspective. Since my interest was in Christian education from a black perspective, I selected a Christian school that was designed to meet the needs of black children in the inner city.

During my brief visit, I observed the chapel service, a variety of classes, and the campus. I also interviewed the principal, students, and instructors, using questions I developed prior to the visit along with ones that emerged spontaneously.

The school impressed me in several ways. In 1993 it became a fully accredited inner-city school, organized and sponsored by a black church as part of its ministry. Founded twenty-three years previously with only one student and one teacher, the school had grown to a current enrollment of approximately four hundred fifty students (three hundred twenty-five families) and twenty black teachers. The students were quiet and attentive in chapel as well as in the classroom. They played cooperatively with one another on the playground. The students listened, followed the instructions for each lesson, and raised their hands to respond to questions. They allowed other students to speak uninterruptedly and waited for their turn to respond. Teachers then praised the children for good work and good behavior. Additionally, the school's pedagogical practice reflected the school's commitment to "the principle of Academic Excellence, in an unashamedly Christian environment."[2] The principal noted that the aim of the school was to maintain a cooperative and supportive relationship with parents, teachers, and students. For instance, parents were expected to review and sign their child's homework every night. They were also encouraged to consult with the principal and teachers regarding any concerns. Furthermore, students were encouraged to interact directly with the principal and teachers as needed.

I was surprised to find that the classroom pictures portrayed biblical characters as white. In addition, the school used a Eurocentric approach to the Scriptures as well as to the overall classroom procedures. For example, the children were given scriptures to learn individually by rote. In contrast, Paul Hill identifies an African-centered pedagogy that stresses group learning, whereby requirements are mastered together. Children begin and complete a task together while supporting one another throughout the process.[3] Yet, from what I observed, these educational practices were not in use. Furthermore, no mention was made of the black presence in the Bible. What a disappointment! How could this happen in a predominantly black school that claimed to embrace as well as promote the African heritage?

Since this was a black school sponsored by a black church, with mostly black American students and teachers, I expected to see the explicit reflection of the black experience in teaching methods, classroom procedures, and visual aids. Overall, this was not the case. It is true that various components of the school reflected, implicitly, the black experience as in the case of references by one or two teachers to black role models and contributions to a particular field of study and to Christian doctrine. However, the black experience was neither expressly incorporated in the overall educational process nor in the presentation of biblical material.

Cain Hope Felder sheds light on what I saw when he highlights the influence of European cultures on biblical interpretation. He says, "Throughout Western history the authority of the Bible has been predicated upon the tacit assumption of the preeminence of European cultures."[4] Felder maintains that African Americans, African Asiatic, Asian, and Hispanic people have typically been viewed as secondary to the ancient biblical narratives and that, historically, the standard by which we read and interpret the Bible has been shaped by the dominant culture.[5]

Although there is clear evidence of the presence and participation of black people in the Bible itself, many Eurocentric church officials and scholars still ignore the contributions of black people. Consequently, these contributions have been distorted, reinterpreted, and reimaged to communicate Eurocentric characters, standards, and values.[6] Unfortunately, many black Americans have embraced and incorporated these distortions in their Bible study, worship, and religious practices. Some black churches still display pictures that portray Jesus with long blonde hair and blue eyes; and members of these congregations often become offended when asked to remove these pictures or to replace them with a black image of Jesus. They have accepted an image of Jesus that was created by the dominant culture and resist other images that may be more representative of their own experiences and culture.

Felder's insightful discussion emphasizes the impact of Western culture on black people. He clearly illustrates how black Americans have been virtually stripped of their heritage, indoctrinated with a Eurocentric worldview, and led to believe that anything Eurocentric is better than anything black. Thus, the very presence and contribution of black people, not only in the Bible but also throughout social history, have been devalued, dehumanized, and denied. This reality has perpetuated black people's self-hatred, lack of respect for one another, black-on-black violence, and a systematic denial of black personhood.

Amos Wilson further illumines Felder's argument regarding the impact of Western culture on black people. In *Black-On-Black Violence,* Wilson presents a horrifying portrait of the social and cultural dynamics that are responsible for perpetuating black-on-black violence in America. Wilson's main focus rests on the psychodynamics of white supremacy and how it has become the root cause of black-on-black violence.[7] Wilson maintains that "in the dominant white American consciousness the African male is existentially guilty," which implies that he is guilty by simply being alive.[8] In a sense, this inherent expectation of guilt creates a "self-fulfilling prophecy" that is played out in the black male psyche and eventually in his actions.[9]

What is most striking about Wilson's discussion is his portrayal of the devastating reality of the system of black self-annihilation and the deep sense of hopelessness black Americans experience. Although Wilson offers some helpful recommendations for the preservation and empowerment of the black community, the question remains whether there is any hope.[10] The answer can be a resounding "yes" if the church offers hope of communal and moral formation for black Americans who have been cast adrift in a violent and seemingly hopeless society. Such a formation is, in fact, wisdom-centered.

The purpose of this chapter is twofold. First, I will reflect on two dominant themes in the work of Grant Shockley, noted black Christian educator and religionist, that support black Americans' rootedness in their wisdom-forming, rich heritage. Second, I will build on these themes to propose a wisdom-directed model of educational ministry that draws on resources in black culture and tradition and that promotes the preservation and celebration of black Christian faith and heritage. The proposed model advances wisdom formation through a holistic approach that embraces the triple heritage composed of African, black American, and Christian roots.[11] The model also proposes that the historical music of black people in America called spirituals is a vehicle for experiencing, expressing, and teaching the triple heritage.[12]

Themes in Grant Shockley's Work

Two dominant themes in the scholarly work of Grant Shockley are important to a discussion of wisdom formation through educational ministry in black churches. The first theme centers on the role of Christian education in the black church. The second theme pertains to liberation theology and Christian education.

The Role of Christian Education in Considering Wisdom Formation

According to Grant Shockley, Christian education is central to the black church.[13] However, Shockley observes that black church Christian education is often deficient in meeting the growing needs of congregations. His in-depth historical analysis of Christian education showed, even though the Sunday school continues to be the most common form of Christian education for black people, this mode of Christian education is largely ineffective in reaching black Americans of all ages.[14] While some churches have improved over the years, many Sunday school programs in black churches still reflect findings of the 1933 study of Benjamin E. Mays and Joseph W. Nicholson: (1) poor attendance; (2) declining enrollment of children and youth; (3) predominant use of uniform rather than graded curriculum resources; (4) lack of pastoral support; (5) adult domination of youth programs; and (6) traditional Sunday schools based on white Protestant church models.[15] My own experiences corroborate the findings. I have also discovered inordinate reliance on the lecture method and reading printed materials that results in passive participation with little time for exploration and reflection. The tendency to place heavy emphasis on Christian doctrine without attention to the black heritage is also problematic.

The lack of variety in teaching methods and techniques is not particular to black churches. But I am concerned that uses of these approaches in black churches override adoption of rich sources of wisdom from the black oral tradition, such as music, dance, poetry, ritual, proverbs, metaphors, stories, and historical accounts. Black heritage celebrations incorporate these sources, especially during worship and various activities on special days. However, sources of wisdom from the black oral tradition are not incorporated in classroom endeavors on a regular basis. Moreover, there seems to be difficulty in helping participants see the implications of lessons for wise holistic living with its personal, spiritual, and social character.

The religious education movement's emphasis on social involvement and new approaches to Christian education, and the civil rights/black power movement challenged the black church not only to affirm its uniqueness but also to take an active role in addressing the concerns of the black community.[16] To address the challenge, some black churches strengthened their Christian education programs by emphasizing justice and liberation, social and ethical responsibility, community involvement, self-help and self-reliance, self-identity and self-esteem, and indigenous modes of religious expression.[17]

For Shockley, Christian education should enable black Americans to celebrate growth in their faith while affirming their cultural uniqueness and distinctive journey. This perspective helps frame wisdom formation as a process wherein black Americans deepen their Christian faith by coming to know and celebrate who they are as unique creations of God. Wisdom formation is about the development of positive self-knowledge and affirmation.

Liberation Theology and Wisdom Formation

Another dominant theme in Shockley's scholarship is black liberation theology.[18] Shockley emphasizes the essential relationship between black liberation theology and Christian education and makes clear the important role of both in the fight for liberation. He also maintains that black theology confronts both black and white churches alike to participate not simply in the liberation of oppressed black Americans, but also in the liberation of all oppressed minorities.[19] However, his particular challenge to the black church is pertinent to my concern for wisdom formation in black Christian education.

Shockley raises two questions, *Why have Christian education in the black church at all?* and *What are the guidelines?* Concerning the first question, he cites the need to develop a curriculum that focuses on the black experience and that affirms freedom, personhood, and hope. He maintains that this curriculum can empower black Americans to strive for liberation and can provide practical tools for civil rights activity.[20] In response to the second question, Shockley offers guidelines for developing a Christian education paradigm that is informed by black theology. These guidelines arise out of the daily challenges faced by black Americans in their ongoing struggle for survival in an oppressive society.[21]

Shockley's view is affirmed in Paul Nichols's assertion that theology and Christian education are interrelated and should "be relevant to the experience of the learner."[22] Thus, black theology should be at the center of black Americans' wisdom formation. I would also widen Shockley's and Nichols's viewpoints to include a womanist perspective that embodies the unique experience of black American women. The inclusion of this perspective is essential to a holisticly focused wisdom formation. The ends toward which this kind of wisdom formation point are black Americans' meaningful relationship with God, their ability to address the holistic needs of all within their communities, their embrace of positive self-worth and pride in their rich cultural heritage, and their sense of empowerment to bring about liberation and social change. The union of black theology, womanist theology, and Christian education is important to wisdom formation and black churches' reclamation of a prophetic voice.

As part of his liberation emphasis, Shockley also identifies the need for a liberation/ praxis model of Christian education in black churches, called the Intentional Engagement Model, that builds on the work of James Cone, Paulo Freire, and Gayraud Wilmore. The model highlights self-awareness, social awareness, social analysis, transformation, praxis, and community involvement. Like Freire, Shockley believes that education is never neutral. It either inhibits or enables liberation.[23] Shockley's model stimulates critical reflection on systems and structures that inhibit liberation, and seeks to empower black Americans' decisions to act concretely for social change.

Shockley's model suggests that the result of wisdom formation should be wise decisions and wise action, meaning those decisions and actions that contribute to black people's liberation from oppressive life conditions and to transformed and wholeness-producing existence. Moreover, his paradigm shows that wise decisions and wise action cannot happen without black people's critical consciousness of and reflection on the realities of their lives, sources of these realities, and the resources to address the realities.

Toward a Wisdom-forming Educational Ministry Through Cultural Rootedness

Shockley's scholarly endeavors point to an educational ministry from a black American perspective that is committed both to reclaiming and building valuable wisdom-forming resources found within our culture and tradition. Implicit in the themes of his work is the view that attention to wisdom formation today for the sake of present and future wise decision making must build on wisdom of the past. And in order to preserve the rich heritage of black Americans, to teach black children the truth about their history, and to provide a holistic ministry within the black community, black churches must be intentional about developing a curriculum that incorporates these resources. In his article entitled "Christian Education: A Black Church Perspective," James H. Harris accents the import of black Americans' knowing their heritage:

> The church must develop programs to enable black children and adults to become culturally literate, teaching the importance of Harriet Tubman, Sojourner Truth, W.E.B. DuBois, Carter G. Woodson, Nat Turner, Malcolm X, Martin Luther King, Jr., and the countless others who have labored for freedom and justice. We need to learn our own history and the value of our contributions to the development of society and the quest for freedom.[24]

Harris's discussion is helpful because he challenges black churches to take an active role in providing biblical teachings while incorporating the black American heritage, including current social concerns, throughout the ministry of the church. He goes on to suggest that this Afrocentric approach must encompass all aspects of the church's ministry, such as worship, choir rehearsals and performances, outreach activities, auxiliary/board meetings, evangelism, and discipleship. Cooperation from both the church and community is needed to carry out this endeavor.

One black American scholar who is breaking new ground in the area of Christian education is Anne S. Wimberly, who is coeditor of this volume. In her earlier book, *Soul Stories: African American Christian Education*, Wimberly introduces an innovative approach to Christian education that centers on the experiences of black people and embraces the oral tradition of storytelling. This contemporary model of Christian education is unique in that it reclaims a vital part of black culture.[25]

Like Harris, Wimberly emphasizes the need for churches to incorporate black history as well as concerns for social action into their educational ministry endeavors. Although Harris cites examples of churches that are teaching black history and taking an active role in addressing communal concerns, he does not offer a model for doing educational ministry from a black perspective. Wimberly, on the other hand, offers a new paradigm for doing Christian education. She explores the themes of liberation, vocation, and ethical decision making through story-linking, a process she defines as tying together personal stories, biblical stories, and faith heritage stories from the black tradition.[26]

Joseph V. Crockett is another black scholar whose work makes a significant contribution to the field of Christian education. Like Harris and Wimberly, Crockett gives pivotal attention to teaching scriptures in light of the unique experiences and traditions of black Americans. In his book *Teaching Scripture from an African American Perspective*, Crockett emphasizes cultural integrity, which he defines as a "respect for the particular experiences and traditions of African Americans."[27] Although Crockett does not develop a paradigm for a Christian education program as Wimberly does, he does introduce four strategies for teaching Scripture in a black context. These strategies are: (1) the story strategy, which accents the oral tradition of storytelling in the African American community; (2) the exile strategy, which examines the impact of forced relocation and bondage of African American people; (3) the sanctuary strategy, which explores the communal characteristics of worship in the African American community; and (4) the exodus strategy, which stimulates critical social reflection and involvement.[28]

The work of these Christian educators is promising because it highlights the importance of educational ministry programs that are culturally sensitive, that combine biblical teachings with black history, and that promote social action within the community.

These scholars' work clearly points to an ethnic cultural orientation that is rich with wisdom and that is useful in the necessary role of black churches in assuring black Christians' wisdom formation.

Yet, while the current literature is helpful, I build upon it by including a Pan-African perspective, which focuses on our triple heritage. If black churches are to be serious about black American Christians' forming wisdom, then I believe it is essential that these churches delve deeply into our heritage, which necessarily means connecting with our roots in Africa, in the Diaspora, and in Christianity. The African proverb, a form of wisdom also familiar to the Judeo-Christian tradition and with which this chapter began, beautifully summarizes this notion. To reiterate, that proverb asserts, "To go back to tradition is the first step forward." Nsenga Warfield-Coppock sheds light on the proverb by stating the following:

> The Akan tradition exemplifies this ancient wisdom with the symbol of the [Sankofa] bird. This bird . . . has a long neck which stretches backward to its tail. It stands on three steps and the words that go with this symbol are "go and fetch it." To go back to the ancient wisdom of our African ancestors we can learn what is in front of us and what it is that we should be doing—our ancestors will lead the way if only we let them.[29]

The wisdom of this African proverb reminds us that as we return to our historical roots we can learn much about the rich faith tradition that is uniquely ours. As we embrace this tradition, we will gain valuable insight into our heritage, our faith tradition, and our understanding of who we are as black African people in the Diaspora.

Janice Hale further stresses this point: "In order to understand faith in African American culture, we must explore and analyze the roots of African American culture in general, and we must consider the religious experience of African Americans by beginning with the African heritage."[30] She goes on to cite Jack Daniel and Geneva Smitherman, who agree that beginning with African heritage is essential since black American culture is strongly influenced and "colored" by a traditional African worldview.[31] Likewise, in his book, *The Spirituality of African Peoples*, Peter Paris convincingly argues for the recognition of the "African factor" when he states, "The African American experience cannot be fully understood apart from its ongoing connectedness with the religious and moral ethos of its African homeland."[32]

Based on this discussion, I submit that educational ministry from a black American perspective can foster black Americans' wisdom formation by making possible their engagement in a holistic curriculum that incorporates a triple-heritage approach, drawing upon the resources from African, black American, and Christian cultures. While there are numerous resources that could inform a curriculum that is grounded in the triple heritage, I suggest a model that focuses on the historical music of black Americans called spirituals, because all three aspects of the triple heritage have informed them. African traditional music has influenced the rhythm, worldview, and spontaneous nature of the spirituals. Black people's experience of slavery gave birth to this music in the secret religious meetings, the work environment, and the harsh realities of bondage. Christianity has inspired them, revealing the faith of a people who have endured great hardships and oppression. The spirituals, therefore, form a point of intersection where the three components of the triple-heritage come together and where reflection on the triple heritage can begin.

Spirituals as a Wisdom-formation Resource

Spirituals can easily be incorporated into Christian education curricula. Since an effective educational ministry will undergird all aspects of the church's ministry, the spirituals are a particularly good resource for use in choirs, Sunday schools, prayer meetings, auxiliary board meetings, outreach programs, worship services, and other ongoing and special events. The formation of a discerning and wise-acting people of God is the concern for every church endeavor; and in light of this interest, triple-heritage resources such as the spirituals can be used to expose the wisdom contained in them. The spirituals are resources that disclose the wisdom of black forebears. This music reveals these forebears' cooperative efforts to promote education, unity, protection, and liberation; and uses of these songs in wisdom-directed education can have the effect of undergirding participants' wisdom formation by

- building their self-esteem,
- enhancing their spiritual growth,
- stimulating their critical reflection, and
- motivating their active participation within the community.

By Christian educators' intentional use of spirituals in educational ministry, then, black Americans can gain not simply insight into their African roots, black American history, and Christian faith, but also guidance that can help them to live wisely with positive self-hood and hope.

Planning for a Triple-heritage Model of Wisdom Formation

Black American Christians have a unique triple heritage that encompasses their African, black American, and Christian roots. As Africans, black Americans can draw upon the rich heritage and wisdom of the motherland (such as tribal customs, naming ceremonies, rituals, music, dance, literature, family structure, and so much more). As black Americans, black Christians can draw upon the legacy of "sheroes" and heroes who have literally built this country. And, as Christians, black persons can draw from the foundation of their faith.

Doing so makes possible their drawing from rich sources of wisdom. But it also requires planning for a triple-heritage model of wisdom-revealing and wisdom-forming Christian education. What, precisely, does *triple heritage* mean, and what are the characteristics of the model, the content and process of teaching, and the nature of curriculum resources?

The Triple Heritage. The triple heritage is defined as African, black American, and Christian. African heritage challenges black Americans to reclaim African history, culture and geography as their ancestral heritage. Black American heritage illumines the experiences and contributions of black Americans in the United States. Christian heritage affirms Jewish and Christian traditions while also celebrating the distinctiveness of black American Christianity.

The triple heritage is a unit with three vital components that together make up a unique whole. These components are closely related and intimately intertwined. Each has essential elements that reveal its place of origin, distinctive characteristics, traditions, cultures, and histories that can be identified and traced. The components engage in a dynamic relationship. They draw upon one another. They flow out of one another and they build upon one another. Each offers a valuable and distinctive contribution to the black American Christian heritage and, together, they make up a holistic view of that heritage.[33]

Characteristics. At least four characteristics describe a triple-heritage wisdom-forming model of educational ministry in the black church that centers on spirituals: communal, creative, critical, and cooperative.

- *Communal.* The wisdom-forming process is not an individualized one. Rather, the formation of a positive sense of personhood, hope, and liberative action happens in community. Consequently, the spirituals, which were created and sung in community, are used to inspire a sense of community in the educational process that aims toward wisdom formation. This formation comes through call and response, a common dialogical form of the spirituals. The leader begins the exchange with a lead phrase or question that communicates a wisdom-oriented narrative to be remembered, considered, and affirmed. The group or congregation enters the dialogue by responding to the lead phrases with statements that either echo a part of the lead phrase, answer a question raised in the lead phrase, or expand the wisdom narrative. The following is an example:

Leader: Didn't my Lord deliver Daniel,
Response: Deliver Daniel, deliver Daniel?
Leader: Didn't my Lord deliver Daniel,
Response: And why not-a everyone?
Leader: God delivered Daniel from the lion's den,
Response: Jonah from the belly of the whale,
Leader: And the Hebrew children from the fiery furnace,
Response: And why not everyone?[34]

In wisdom-oriented educational ministry, this particular example becomes a means by which students and teachers can enter into critical reflection on the wisdom of God that undergirds wise communal action. Songs like this one promote communal dialogue, encouraging both students and teachers to participate fully in the educational process. Since each person brings something valuable to the dialogue, anyone may begin the call and response at any time, engaging the entire community in a dynamic exchange of ideas and experiences.

• *Creative.* The spirituals offer a creative means by which wisdom formation can occur. This music invites novel consideration of the connections between past and present life circumstances; and the music engages persons' imagination and ways of thinking and acting in light of those circumstances through its disclosure of stories, ideas, injunctions, and values. Moreover, Zora Neale Hurston noted that the spirituals themselves are always in the process of creation.[35] Since a common characteristic of the spirituals is improvisation, they can be shaped and reshaped to accommodate a particular situation or event. For instance, the words in the spiritual, "Don't Let Nobody Turn You 'Round" were changed to "Don't Let Segregation Turn You Around" for use during and after the 1960s Civil Rights movement. The important point here is that wisdom-forming Christian education that utilizes spirituals in the triple-heritage model is, by its very nature, an ongoing process of creation. In this process, songs may be refashioned and infused with new meanings; and through them, the participants may form fresh and insightful approaches to life's realities and challenges. Both the resources used in the triple heritage and the participants who use them are shaped and reshaped throughout the wisdom-forming process.

• *Critical.* Wisdom-formation processes necessarily entail critical analytical components. The uses of spirituals are helpful in this regard, especially those possessing dual or hidden meanings. Spirituals of this kind were often used by black people during the slave era to communicate secret messages with one another without being detected by their masters.

Grounded in African tradition, this feature allowed the slaves to relate words of insult, history, wisdom, humor, and critique. For example, the words "ev'rybody talkin' 'bout heav'n ain't goin' there"[36] were often used to mock slaveholders and to critique their religious hypocrisy. Employing songs of this nature in a triple-heritage wisdom formation model of Christian education encourages participants to critique their experiences of hurt and injustice while also reflecting on their personal feelings about those experiences. The songs are channels not simply for forging critical consciousness of oppressive circumstances and structures, but for empowering black Americans to be self-critical as well, and to decide on liberating actions that can lead to change and human wholeness. In short, the triple-heritage model in Christian education recognizes the link between critical consciousness, empowerment, and wisdom formation. And the use of spirituals in this model is a key means of stimulating both critical consciousness and empowerment to act wisely or with intentionality and hope in the oftentimes difficult situations of life.

• *Cooperative.* Wisdom formation from a black American perspective requires attention to the kind of self-initiated and cooperative effort that appears in spirituals such as "Oh, Freedom," "Walk Together, Children," and "We Shall Walk Through the Valley." The importance of these kinds of songs lies in their disclosure of and invitation to black people today to explore the ethic of unified determination that undergirded black people's past wise action during their struggle for liberation and human wholeness. Through these songs, the triple-heritage model of wisdom formation seeks to bring about black people's cooperative action that hold potential for transformation and change within and beyond their communities. Moreover, the emphasis on cooperative action in wisdom formation processes is designed to evoke deliberate attention in Christian education groups to their role and, in fact, the whole church's role as change agents in local and global communities.

Content and Process. Every aspect of the triple heritage contributes to the content and teaching process of a triple-heritage wisdom formation model. Although there are numerous educational qualities embodied in the spirituals (for example, dialogue, spontaneity, rhythm, narrative, nature, and ritual) that can function as lenses to explore meanings of wisdom for living, I want to focus specifically on narrative at this point.

Many spirituals tell the stories of biblical characters and events. Examples of these spirituals are "Didn't It Rain," "Go Down, Moses," "Joshua Fit de Battle of Jericho," "Little David, Play on Your Harp," "Ezek'el Saw de Wheel," "Didn't My Lord Deliver Daniel?" "Wake Up, Jonah!" and "Go, Tell It on the Mountain." These narratives remind us today of the importance of story in the oral culture of the ancestral African homeland and in the history of black people in this country.

Most important, however, these storied songs are channels for considering in Christian education how previous generations of black people understood God to be, how Scripture informed their understanding, and what this understanding meant for their practice of wisdom. Likewise, the stories invite our discernment of who God is to us today, what we glean from the Bible about God today, and how this understanding links with our becoming wise people of God. For example, during the era of slavery, black people sang the Exodus story in the song "Go Down, Moses":

> When Israel was in Egypt's land: Let my people go;
> Oppressed so hard they could not stand, Let my people go.
> Go down, Moses, 'Way down in Egypt land,
> Tell ole Pharaoh, Let my people go.
> Oh, let us all from bondage flee, Let my people go;
> And let us all in Christ be free, Let my people go.[37]

Through this song black people disclosed their identification with the children of Israel and a "spirituality of wisdom" that centered on their belief in a God who identified with their suffering, who would not forsake them, and who would one day liberate them from bondage. The question may be asked, *In what ways does this biblical story, the slaves' interpretation of it, and their understanding of God speak to black people today in the midst of challenges of racism, sexism, classism, poverty, and other forms of oppression?*

In reciting the Exodus story in song, black people in slavery also expressed a covert form of resistance to bondage. Jon Michael

Spencer notes that "behind the mask of the spirituals was authentic *confrontation* and *conflict*."[38] By examining the origins of using coded messages, we can gain insight into African worldviews, customs, practices, and beliefs. These aspects of African heritage may offer wisdom that comes from exploring values undergirding confrontation and conflict, the nature and timing of confrontation and conflict, and persons' willingness to engage in and undergo consequences of confrontation and conflict. In short, there is a theology of wisdom revealed through this spiritual and others that may assist our analysis and response to contemporary challenges.

Curriculum Resources. Curriculum resources for a triple-heritage wisdom formation model should include several elements. First, these resources must fully embody the triple heritage and present the heritage in a balanced fashion throughout the curriculum. Second, resources must draw from the wellspring of music, including but not restricted to the spirituals, stories, proverbs, ritual, dance, art, literature, folktales, and metaphors that are found in the black American Christian tradition. Third, resources must tap the rich origins and contents of the religious lives of historical and contemporary black Americans, including sources that inform their music (for example, the Bible, belief systems, and worldview). Fourth, the resources must present positive images of black Americans. And, finally, resources must be "highly interactive as well as engage various senses, abilities, and cultural forms."[39]

CHAPTER 3

Forming Wisdom Through Cross-generational Connectedness

Anthony G. Reddie

Young bud no know when berry ripe on mountain.
(The young depend on the elders.)
— *Jamaican proverb*

This chapter builds on my work over many years with African Caribbean young people undertaken through Methodist and Anglican churches in the Birmingham region of Britain.[1] The work connected younger and older generations so that the wisdom found in the oral tradition of the elders could be shared. I found that this kind of cross-generational connectedness gave young people a valuable basis for their wisdom formation and hope.[2] This chapter is about the nature and importance of this approach to wisdom formation. There is increasing awareness among black people of African descent in the Diaspora that accessing historical faith and wisdom is necessary to confront change and challenge in the twenty-first century. The young especially seek wisdom found in cultural values and a view of life illuminated by the Spirit of God that transcends time, context, and oppression.

A Case for Oral Tradition in Forming Wisdom

In the last chapter, Yolanda Smith highlighted the richness of wisdom from the black heritage that is shared orally through music. Whether through music or other means, the oral tradition has been a dominant means by which black people in Africa and the African Diaspora have shared and formed wisdom. Fred Lofton maintains that the oral tradition has been essential to black people's surviving the dehumanizing experiences of slavery and maintaining a valued identity in whatever location they were found.[3] This oral tradition was passed down in cross-generational contexts through storytelling and has provided a necessary filter to the disinformation of demonized selfhood of black people.

Historically, Christian formation among black people happened through an oral tradition expressed in Sunday worship and through family instruction and storytelling during the remainder of the week.[4] Through these dual approaches, black people formed a spiritual and moral wisdom, including deep convictions and commitments needed to shape a life of meaning and purpose, as well as attitudes, behaviors, and skills needed to act with integrity in and on behalf of the community.

Written Christian education curricula that emphasize ocular versus oral pedagogies are more recent innovations in the black church. Grant Shockley's historical research shows that text-based Christian education programs only came into prominence in the black church in the twentieth century.[5] Prior to that time, an oral tradition centered on individual and corporate experience, expressed through storytelling and proverbial wisdom, was the usual approach.

Over time, text-based teaching and learning have become overemphasized. And, while the legitimacy of this route to wisdom formation cannot be denied, it has tended to mask the central importance of oral communication and its power to inspire, transform, and energize black people. There continues to be the need to reclaim the oral means of promoting wisdom formation; and there is critical need for person-to-person cross-generational sharing to make it happen.

Making Orality Come Alive Today

Ella Mitchell's reference to Christian faith being "caught, not taught" inspired my earlier thinking about orality in black life, and my first attempt to investigate the oral tradition of African Caribbean people in 1996.[6] I explored the fascinating area of proverbial wisdom, and created materials focused on this wisdom. One series of materials addressed the theme of maternal wisdom.[7] In the introduction to that material I wrote the following: "In African and Caribbean societies, where many of the cultural values and traditions are preserved and passed on orally through stories and experience, the mother's informal role as 'educator' of the child remains hugely important."[8]

While piloting the activities that focused on life issues and themes emerging in the African Caribbean community, I became convinced of the power of orality in cross-generational interactions, and its effect on wisdom formation. An example was given by one of my co-researchers, a Sunday school teacher named Jackie.

Jackie had selected and presented to a regular group of African Caribbean children in her church a contemporary *proverbial* folktale called "The Wisdom of Soulful Sister 'P,' " which I had written.[9] My intention in writing the folktale had been to highlight ways in which wisdom and understanding have often been passed down through succeeding generations by wise matriarchs within the diverse communities of the African Diaspora. I wanted to enable African Caribbean children to gain a sense of the dynamics and power of cross-generational discourse between black elders, especially grandmothers, and their descendants. I also wanted to portray black narrative and experience as being an important repository of wisdom. Moreover, I wanted to present the elderly African woman as an essential bearer of wisdom in the white British-dominated society where there are far too few black role models and heroes/sheroes, and where black people are almost exclusively pathologized and demonized.

The story tells of a black woman who is the oldest and wisest person in her African village. When a number of individuals in the village struggle to answer questions pertaining to their lives, they all seek the wisdom of Soulful Sister P. In the story, Soulful Sister P has a particularly close rapport with the young children in the village. The advice she gives them is invaluable in enabling them to understand the need to be "wise" in their dealings with others and the world as a whole.

Jackie's report of telling the story to her group of children during a cross-racial worship service indicated that not only did the children exhibit lively response, but the adults also joined in as well, particularly in repeating Soulful Sister P's prayer. Jackie indicated that a picture of this praying matriarch punctuated the storytelling and helped the listeners imagine the person about whom the story was being told. Jackie concluded that the impact of the story lay in its disclosure of "an example of a very wise person who had a lot to teach us about how to live our lives." Jackie also indicated that the story ensured that the white people present received a positive image of the wise black lady in the story. Jackie queried, "If left to the imagination, how many would have [had] the right image, I wonder?"

Opportunity and Challenge to Oral Sharing Within the Extended Family

A number of my conversations with African Caribbeans have underscored the important wisdom-forming function of stories that are shared with the young by black elders in extended family contexts. Many young third-generation black Caribbeans in Britain have learned about their ancestors and antecedents of their cultural identity by listening to the elders' stories and experiences. However, what troubled me about this discourse was the sporadic nature of these storytelling events. Many older African Caribbean elders spoke of their embarrassment and insecurity in sharing their experiences and wisdom for fear of impeding the ability of these younger people to become truly British.

I have noted, as well, that within the contemporary literature associated with "race," ethnicity, and culture in Britain, a number of commentators have highlighted explicit and covert forces exerted by the British state to compel and cajole black migrants to assimilate and integrate.[10] The familiar aphorism "When in Rome, do as the Romans do" is often repeated in order to remind black people in Britain that the only legitimate basis on which we can exist in this country is by a wholesale negation of self. We are to embrace white English ways of being and relating. It seems that black people in Britain are expected to repudiate their culture, narratives, and experiences (all of which are the raw materials that produce collective and corporate wisdom) in favor of alleged superior values of so-called "indigenous people."

The program of planned, cross-generational conversations begun by me between African Caribbean elders and their descendants has been a means of countering strictures of integration and assimilation. The next section presents two examples of the intentional and exceedingly expressive process of cross-generational wisdom-sharing. One example describes dialogue that occurred in the families of Charlene and Terry, while the other example illustrates a process of cross-generational wisdom-sharing that took place in Jonie's family.

Processes of Cross-generational Wisdom-sharing

I functioned as a guide and participant in the planned process of cross-generational wisdom-sharing with two families, that of Charlene and Terry and their respective parents, and the extended family of Jonie. In both instances, I became aware of similar kinds of content (wisdom-oriented dialogue) and varied interpersonal dynamics occurring in the cross-generational conversation. In both instances, these families' sharing was epitomized by content focused on a kind of spirituality of wisdom. In fact, this same spiritual emphasis in content tended to be repeated in other families who participated in the project.

Inevitably, prayer was at the center of this spirituality of wisdom. The elders were consistent in telling stories of situations calling for conversations with God, and of the absolute necessity of prayer in the lives of faithful Christians in order to continue on in life with hope in spite of hardship or even the very threat to life itself. But the content of wisdom the elders in the families shared also went beyond prayer and included an emphasis on the theme of otherness. This theme became reflected in vivid references to the contributions of African and Caribbean cultures to the ancestral identity of black Caribbeans.

What came across was the importance of the elders' sharing and the young's formation of a profound or wise knowing of their valued "is-ness" that connects with their African and Caribbean ancestry or "other." The message of the elders was that the "is-ness" of our ethnicity, culture, and family identity has its roots in a long history of blood and flesh others in Africa and the Caribbean and to whom we remain linked.

Of course the conversations between the generations contained much more than it is possible to articulate here. However, let me invite you, the reader, into part of a conversation in which I participated with each family. By sharing the parts of the dialogue, I wish to provide a basis for proposing a pedagogical process for guiding cross-generational dialogue aimed toward wisdom formation of the young.

Dialogue in Charlene's and Terry's Families

The participants in this first example of wisdom-sharing dialogue included Charlene, age fifteen, and Terry, age seven at the time of the conversation; Charlene's mother, Diane; Terry's parents, Mel and Mick; and me. I functioned as the facilitator of the process of cross-generational sharing.

The Process Unfolds. I began by asking the three adults for their memories of being nurtured in the Caribbean. Having heard the accounts of Diane, Mel, and Mick, I attempted to ascertain from Charlene and Terry their thoughts and experiences of the Caribbean. The comments of the younger family members were supplemented by the older individuals. These comments were often made in very humorous terms, recounting embarrassing episodes from the recent past. I was struck by the sense of shared experiences between successive generations of African Caribbeans living in Britain. The conversation proceeded as follows:

Anthony. So Charlene, you were born in Birmingham? *(She responds by nodding her head.)* Have you ever been to Jamaica?
Charlene. Yeah.
Anthony. What did you think was the biggest difference between Jamaica and here?
Diane. Shall I tell you what she said?
Mel. Apart from the weather!

Diane. When she got over the initial shock. "Mum, they're black!" *(There is much laughter at this point.)* How old was she then?

Mel. This was the first trip then?

Diane. First trip? Nine? Was it ninety? She was about six. And the first reaction. *(Pause)* I think it's because she's used to seeing a lot of white people. And then you go, and everywhere you go are black people.

Mel. (Interrupting) Especially living in Rowley Regis, innit, where we are? Because not a lot of black people in 'round here. I think in the whole of Rowley there must be about, at a push, probably twenty families, innit? At a push.

Diane. Her first reaction was, I think—apart from, as I said, the heat—was the color of the people. Not that she wasn't used to seeing blacks, you know; but she wasn't used to seeing so many in one place. (More laughter)

Anthony. (To Charlene) When was the last time you went?

Charlene. Hmmm. Two?

Charlene and Diane. Two years ago.

Anthony. What was the biggest difference then? Being a little bit older?

Charlene. I don't know. All the insects and bugs and stuff.

Anthony. (Not quite hearing the first time) All the . . . ?

Charlene. Bugs.

Anthony. Oh yeah. Yeah.

Diane. (Begins to mumble under her breath) The nightmare with the insects.

Charlene. I don't know.

Mel. What about the difference between you as a teenager and the teenagers there?

Diane. There isn't that much difference really.

Charlene. No.

Diane. They're all sort of—

Charlene. (Interrupting) kinda like American.

Diane. Jamaica seems to be very American.

Mick. Of course, it's just 'round the corner.

Mel. That difference isn't really there. But I think as they got older they adapted more to change. Got used to the dogs and cats *(Laughter)* and the cows in the yard a bit more. *(More laughter)*

Anthony. (To Charlene) Did you enjoy yourself?

Charlene. Yes.

Anthony. What was the best thing about it? Being there? All right, not the best thing. Anything. Tell me, anything? Anything that you liked?

Charlene. The beaches. *(Lots of laughter) (Being very ironic)* It's a bit better than Blackpool [a local beach in Britain]. Only a bit better.

Mel. What you mean, a bit better?

Charlene. A tiny bit better than Blackpool.

Mel. Get away. *(More laughter)*

Anthony. So Terry, have you ever been to Jamaica?

Terry. Yeah.

Anthony. Did you like it?

Terry. Yeah.

Anthony. What did you like?

Terry. Going on the motorbike.

Anthony. (In astonishment) Motorbike? Oh gosh. What was the weather like?

Terry. Hot.

Anthony. Hotter than over here?

Terry. No . . . yes.

Charlene. I don't remember it being hotter over there. Oh, I get what you said now. It is hot.

Diane. "Gimme my sunglasses, Mum, as soon as we get off the plane. "Where's my sunglasses, where's my sunglasses?" *(More laughter)* Blinded by the sun. "I can't see, I can't take it."

Mel. That's true, when we went two years ago, innit? Hmm . . . I spent quite a lot of time with my eyes squinched up. And even with sunglasses on. I think next time I go I shall have to invest in a decent pair of sunglasses. Yes, it's a bit hard on the eyes when you're not accustomed to it. *(More laughter)*

Pedagogical Insights. The process by which black youth form wisdom in cross-generational dialogue requires attention to experiences that contribute to their valuing their identity and culture in the midst of alienating circumstances. Of particular importance is young people's hearing their parents' and other elders' childhood stories that situate the young people in another time and place to stimulate the young people's appreciation of their cultural roots. Movement toward this end entails a deliberate starting point and interaction between adults and young people around the place of ancestry.

The dialogical process did not end with this interchange. In fact, there was considerably more interaction focused on the childhood experiences of the parents, and the youths' responses to them.

The starting point with Charlene, Terry, and their parents was my invitation to the adults to recall significant events in their early lives in the Caribbean, followed by my posing questions to the youth to elicit responses from them. The questions were designed to help them to "see" themselves in the other environment of their parents and ancestors. Such a process may not necessarily be an altogether smooth undertaking. In the dialogue recounted above, Charlene and Terry gave abbreviated answers; and the adults often volunteered answers to questions posed to the youth. Helpful continuation of the dialogue may mean calling out the name of the person to whom a question is being presented or re-presented.

As the conversation progressed beyond the opening frame, I was struck by Charlene's knowledge of her mother's formative years in rural Jamaica. Charlene recognized and accepted that her mother's upbringing might have been more tranquil and less complicated than her own childhood. Moreover, she voiced her awareness that her formative experiences in Britain lacked the acute poverty of her mother's early years. The shared event allowed Charlene and, to a lesser extent, also Terry to embrace the Caribbean as a symbolic and signified resource for their existential quest for a positive self-identity.

Dialogue in Jonie's Family

The African Caribbean context of cross-generational dialogue to be discussed in this section differs from the preceding one in that it includes extended family members. Jonie, an African Caribbean woman was in her fifties at the time I met her. Jonie was a Sunday school leader in a Methodist church situated in the northern part of Birmingham. Her granddaughter Debbie, and two grandnieces named Shona and Bonnie, joined her in the dialogue. Debbie was six years old. Shona and Bonnie were eight and six years old, respectively.

In contrast to my commencing with the parents of Charlene and Terry, my starting point in this extended family conversation was the three young children. My reason for beginning with them was to model before the grandparent and grandaunt a way of engaging the young in intergenerational dialogue. I had also learned from the elders that they had engaged in storytelling with the children. I wanted to know what the children had gleaned from those stories as a means of reinforcing the importance of storytelling times. I began by asking the children their thoughts about Jamaica, the birthplace of their grandmother and grandaunt.

Anthony. (To the three girls) So tell me, have you ever heard of Jamaica?
The Girls. Yeah.
Anthony. You all have. So Debbie, what have you heard about Jamaica?
Debbie. That they talk different, like, [with an] accent.
Anthony. Yeah.
Debbie. And they play loads of drums.
Anthony. Ah. They play drums! And what is the weather like?
Debbie. Hot.
Anthony. Hot? Have you ever been to Jamaica?
Debbie. No.
Anthony. Seen pictures?
Debbie. Yep.
Anthony. Okay. Have you ever heard anyone speak with the accent?
Debbie. No. Sorry.
Anthony. No, no, it's okay. *(To Bonnie)* Bonnie, what have you heard?
Bonnie. I've heard that it's really hot and . . . errm, errm . . . they grow lots of crops, and they don't get that much rain. And they've got . . . errm . . . they live in hotels, and they're really, really posh. And that . . . errm . . . the schools are quite big. The end!
Anthony. Shona!
Shona. When the crops grow, [the people] have carnivals and make costumes for a month. And when they've made them, they go on the streets playing drums, and they go *(Begins to sing a well-*

known Caribbean calypso song), "Are you feeling hot, hot, hot" *(The other children begin to join in);* "feeling hot, hot, hot." *(Stops singing)* And with the wavers they go *(Begins to wave her arms in the air, and is followed by her sister and cousin).* And at school, we learnt about carnivals.

Anthony. Okay.

Shona. And the steel band came.

Anthony. And the steel bands came as well? Okay. This question is for anyone now. What do you think is the biggest difference between being in Jamaica and being here? Anyone?

Bonnie. I think the biggest difference is because you've got all kinds of religions in this country, but I think you've got black in Jamaica.

Anthony. Okay. Debbie?

Debbie. I think it's not that hot, and they've got, like, different houses.

Anthony. Okay. That's a good answer. And you, Shona?

Shona. I think they've got big [recording] studios, . . . in Jamaica, I've heard about . . . and you see lots of people in there.

During this brief interchange with the three children, there was a sense of their awareness of the birthplace of their grandmother and grandaunt, and of some aspects of the sociocultural and historical roots of their own identity among others in that place. But there were also clues that point to the need for further conversation and storytelling, particularly with their elders, that could contribute powerfully to the children's wisdom formation.

Pedagogical Insights. Throughout the conversation, the girls focused particularly on music, identifying drums and singing as being integral aspects of Caribbean life. The song sung by Shona, with the accompaniment of her sister and cousin, is by a well-known calypso/Soca singer called The Mighty Sparrow. The song is part of the staple "diet" of most African Caribbean parties, dances, or celebrations. Calypso/Soca music is not usually represented in the repertoire of mainstream popular music in Britain. The inclusion of this music on mainstream commercial radio stations remains limited.

In my continuing conversations with Jonie and her family, I was struck by the extent to which there was an ongoing dialogue between the various members of this intergenerational family. Older family members had constantly shared aspects of the Caribbean history, antecedents, and heritage, thereby highlighting the essential impact it has on the formation of cultural and communal values. I also became aware of the home as a valid and intentional context for educational ministry directed toward wisdom formation.

Importantly, adults should not be reticent to share their early experiences and black history with the young, because this sharing creates a bridge that links the young with the wider ancestral family of Africans in the Diaspora.[11] For example, the communal celebrations referred to in the conversation in Jonie's family are not unlike those occurring in other African and African Diasporan contexts. Wisdom can be gleaned from the African-oriented communal ethic and shared action that became a hallmark of black life in the Caribbean and elsewhere. This wisdom is worthy of the young's embrace. In sharing communal-oriented wisdom, however, it is important for adults to present concrete experiences of communal activity, to engage the young in conversations about the activity, and to explore the importance of the activity with them.

The efforts of adults also need to include inviting young people's perceptions not only about the stories of the Caribbean they share but also about images of the region that appear on white-dominated media. These cross-generational efforts must foster youth's wise knowing of their human worth as well as their internalization and practice of culturally affirming values. At the same time, cross-generational connectedness must stimulate the youth's awareness of differences between sociocultural and historical reality and the clichéd images of the culture appearing on television. For example, fostering this kind of critical thinking through cross-generational conversations about televised images would be an important follow-up to Debbie's, Bonnie's, and Shona's shared perceptions of Jamaican hotel living, which likely derived from televised images of a romantic idyllic Caribbean isle for affluent tourists.

Similarly, an additional cross-generational dialogue is suggested by six-year-old Bonnie's recognition of the difference between a country that is populated predominantly by black people and whose religious life is also black. Pedagogically, the direction of cross-generational dialogue that contributes to wisdom formation would center on what it means to be a black person in a black church and in a black community as well as what it means to be a black person in a predominantly white social context. Wisdom formation entails black children's and youths' seeing black others in black contexts as their relations, as links to their own identity, and contributors to their selfhood through the history and stories of the others. Wisdom formation also consists of black children's and youths' internalization of positive views of themselves and of seeing and acting on their ability to live wholly as selves in their communities.

Guiding Wisdom Formation in Cross-generational Contexts

Whether in households, congregations, or community settings, wisdom formation of black children and youth must be promoted with intentionality. But specific approaches to guiding the process are helpful, especially because of the reluctance of many black adults to share stories for fear of infringing on the lives of the young. In what follows, I will suggest several key approaches that Christian educators, parents, grandparents, and community workers may use to engage black children and youth in cross-generational conversations.

Four strategies begin the engagement:
Mutual invitation. Beginning the kind of cross-generational wisdom formation I am advocating calls for several intentional considerations. One pertains to the relational environment in which guidance of wisdom formation is to occur. It is important that adults and young people enter into wisdom-forming cross-generational communication through a sense of mutual invitation. However, when there has been little prior involvement in this kind of communication in family or church contexts, adults will need to take the lead. Leading entails inviting children and youth into times of storytelling and story-listening and inviting them to tell their own experiences, including those about which they have concerns or questions. Moreover, in the adult-initiated process of sharing, it is important to solicit from the young their feelings about

the shared experiences in which they participate. The intent is to create an open environment that results in young people's expressed desire for it.

Cultural Meal. Pedagogically, a helpful way of developing an affirming environment in which to enter into open conversation is to commence with a cultural meal. Part of the richness of familial sharing arises through the preparation of the meal. In creating time for this activity, the various participants of different ages talk through how they have learned to cook (or not, as the case may be, which is a ripe subject for further conversation) and what the food that is being prepared means to them. Within the African Caribbean context in Britain, this preparation and subsequent eating together might focus on stories surrounding the cultural delights of rice and peas, chicken, ackee and saltfish, cuckoo (cornmeal and maize), and flying fish. In the United States, stories may arise from preparing and partaking of candied yams, fatback, and collard greens.

What we want to happen is the creation of a "safe" environment into which the various participants can enter. Questions pertaining to food and its role in family, community, and history can be supplemented by issues that may be more personal and potentially of greater import. This may lead into concerns surrounding Christian faith, doubt, struggles with hardships and loss, and ending with hope for the future. I must confess here, too, that the importance of food as an occasion for wisdom-forming cross-generational wisdom sharing was affirmed by the film *Soul Food*, which details the family life experiences of a contemporary black American family. The use of films like this one and other illustrative materials offer ways of inspiring the kind of cross-generational connectedness that is so pivotal to wisdom formation of the young.

Experienced Ministry Leadership. A third consideration regards the role of the professional or experienced educational ministry leader. I have found that families often need and are quite open to guidance from experienced leaders who can provide them with approaches and guidance in forging cross-generational connections that result in shared wisdom. Yet it is important that the educational ministry leader give helpful oversight and guidance, and refrain from unhelpful control. I have found that families have most appreciated my modeling for them a process of engaging the young; and this activity may take place either in the homes or in group contexts within the church. It is also exceedingly important to discover from the families the kinds of interactions in which their members typically engage, to encourage them to feel confident about experimenting with new approaches, and to offer suggestions where requested. I have often discovered in families surprising and refreshing cross-generational communication from which the young have clearly received wise counsel and, in turn, have contributed to the adults deepening insights into the lives and approaches to meeting the needs of the young.

Reciprocity. Finally, in relating the earlier story of sharing in Charlene and Terry's family, I pointed to the concern for reciprocity. The important role of educational ministry leaders is to emphasize the imperative use of an open dialogical method between adult and child and to demonstrate this method. There is critical need for a pedagogy that emphasizes the role of adults and children as co-learners. In using this term, I am speaking in prosaic terms of the need for adults to "hear" what their children or grandchildren are saying. This pedagogy is not the same as the kind of one-way discourse entailing "reminiscence work" in which the adult speaks *at* and not *with* the child. In this case, there is very little reciprocity. Nor am I referring to cross-generational discourse in which the adult speaks or answers for the child. In my own work with families, I suggest an alternating approach to conversation. The emphasis is on taking turns and on the skill of listening to the one who is talking. Moreover, when one individual has spoken, the other party may offer a comment, a counterpoint, or a question for clarification or further illumination. No one individual should dominate either the conversation or the other. By inserting these guidelines, it is my intention to ensure that children are (1) heard, and (2) their insights are accepted as valid.

Cultural theories and anthropologists remind us that cultures are neither static nor material entities in and of themselves. Rather, they are constantly being remade. Consequently, it is essential that children be enabled to enter into dialogue with their elders, thereby contributing to the refashioning of communal wisdom. In order to ensure that a reciprocal, dialogical process takes place, it is important that educational ministry leaders who are skilled in interpersonal dynamics are on hand to tool others in these skills and to gently intervene and guide (often the adults) toward reciprocity.

On occasion, I have inserted humor into the proceedings as a means of highlighting the spirited and cheerful nature that wisdom-forming, cross-generational sharing can have. For example, humor has taken the form of my issuing either the adults or the young people a bell. When one party gives far more than one point or begins to dominate the conversation in ways that preclude others' participation, a designated individual can ring the bell and call for a "time out." The use of the bell is limited to situations where there is a great deal of trust and a very relaxed atmosphere between the various participants.

The importance of homogeneous and compact contexts for cross-cultural sharing. From the various attempts to facilitate the formation of wisdom through cross-generational connectedness, I have discovered that the most positive results occur in situations that might be described as "homogeneous" and "compact." These terms refer to cultural contexts, such as the black church and the home setting, where there is a self-sameness and a high degree of continuity, shared cultural values, and experiences of a group of people. Even where there are known generational differences, the existence of cultural commonalities such as physical traits, colloquialisms, and other mannerisms will be recognized and will provide a means of connecting. Commonalities offer an essential starting point for conversations, which allow for cross-generational sharing of proverbial sayings, cultural historical information and values, and emerging ways of living that call for reflection on wisdom.

But, by way of concluding, what has greatly impressed me in the cross-generational processes of sharing in which I have been leader and participant has been my own wisdom formation. In many respects, I believe I have learned more than I have been able to give. Certainly, it has intensified my love and appreciation for that which has been done on my behalf by my parents and numerous ancestors around the world. It is this awareness that I wish to pass on to educational ministry leaders who must surely be on the very journey of wisdom formation toward which we are guiding others.

CHAPTER 4

Singing Hope in the Key of Wisdom: Wisdom Formation of Youth

Evelyn L. Parker

The Lord will make a way somehow, when beneath the cross I bow;
He will take away each sorrow, let him have your burdens now.
                                                              —Thomas A. Dorsey[1]

Black youth are growing up in an age of technological advancement, information explosion, and material gain. Yet, even though these young members of our community seek and will receive benefits from twenty-first-century progress, they also confront devastating problems. Black youth are disproportionately represented among the poor, groups lacking in basic health insurance, the school-aged receiving unsatisfactory education in failing public schools, and those needing improved skills to compete in an ever-demanding marketplace. Moreover, black youth live in a world that is becoming more and more violent, and where they experience the ongoing ravages of racism. These youth also feel criticized and even shunned by older generations within and outside the church because of their distinctive ways of expressing themselves.[2] Where do they find wisdom for their third-millennium sojourn?

In their search for wisdom that is needed to grow with hope, black youth are embracing a popular music heard in public media and are insisting we use it in our churches. Through the genre of hip-hop gospel, they connect with stories of empowerment amidst life's difficulties, and spiritual resources for daily living. The music uniquely continues the role of black music in contributing to black youths' movement toward a valued identity and black Christian wisdom that centers on hope. The song lyrics with which this chapter began is evidence of this tradition.

Thomas A. Dorsey, a sage of gospel music, penned the chorus from "The Lord Will Make a Way Somehow" in the 1940s. This song of hope captures Dorsey's expectation and assurance that God will create possibilities even though present struggles make life seem impossible. Using a metaphor to capture his arduous troubles, Dorsey describes himself as a ship being tossed and battered by angry waves. He questions his actions that could have possibly caused such a raging sea. But he resolves to take courage and expect the Lord to calm the storms of life.[3]

The black slave community sang similar songs of hope two hundred years before Dorsey. The Negro spiritual "Didn't My Lord Deliver Daniel?," to which Yolanda Smith referred in a previous chapter, captures the assurance of deliverance from the egregious trials and tribulations of life. Our enslaved forebears chronicled their tenacious hope and perseverance in difficult times in the song "Keep yo' han' on-a de plow, Hold on! Hold on!"[4] The community continued to pass on the value of the liberative hope of God during the civil rights struggle of the turbulent 1960s. During that time "We Shall Overcome" became a song of expectancy that wove women and men of every ethnicity and class together in locked arms of commitment to freedom. From the mid–1970s to the 1990s, gospel choirs, families, and choral groups sang songs of hope. These vocalists included James Cleveland, Andraé Crouch, Edwin Hawkins, the Winans, and Take Six. The gospel song "Sunday's on the Way," released in 1990 by the group Take Six, celebrates the source of our hope, Jesus Christ, his victory over death, and his resurrection from the grave. The song's title is a metaphor that symbolizes the hope that Jesus Christ brings.

This brief historical review of hope in African American religious music from slavery to the mid-1990s suggests that Christian hope is a central value intimately woven throughout the "wisdom tradition" of the black community. When I use the term "wisdom tradition," I am referring to the lineage of our black forebears to present grandmothers, grandfathers, teens, children, aunts, uncles, cousins, play-mamas, play-daddies, big-daddies, big-mamas, pastors/ preachers/ reverends, deacons, deaconesses, stewards, and stewardesses—all our kin/fictive kin with whatever endearing name we call them—who embody the meaning of black Christian wisdom. Christian wisdom formation is the dynamic process of initiating people into the collective values, beliefs, and practices that the wisdom tradition creates. Christian wisdom formation means learning to live in hope. Hope is the cultivation of expectation, assurance, and confidence in the promises and presence of God made known in Jesus Christ our redeemer and sustainer through the power of the Holy Spirit. Christian wisdom formation is incarnated in all the host of witnesses who accept the teachings and ministry of Jesus Christ, the exemplar of hope. "For in hope we were saved" (Romans 8:24).

In short, Christian hope is intricately woven into the tapestry of the Christian wisdom tradition of the black community; and the foundation for this hope is laid for the black church's ministry with youth through the strong, creative thread that music adds to that tapestry. This chapter will explore briefly Grant Shockley's contributions to the foundations for Christian hope in popular music among black youth. I will then analyze selected hip-hop gospel songs that are popular among today's black teenagers. My intent is to show the presence of historical threads of hope that continue in the music and serve as a reservoir for our youths' wisdom formation.

Foundations of Christian Hope from the Work of Grant Shockley

In the book *Working with Black Youth*, Shockley introduces a theoretical framework for ministry with black youth by tracing the historical task of the North American black church to "understand the religious, social, and educational issues" that influence African American youth ministry.[5] Shockley indicates that Christian Endeavor ·societies in African Methodist

Episcopal, and black Baptist churches were among those organizations emphasizing "commitment, constancy, faithful attendance, and serious Bible study" among its youth.[6] The concern was for addressing our youths' developmental task of becoming physically mature, acquiring skills for adulthood, becoming independent from parents, and negotiating same-sex and opposite-sex relationships.[7]

Who am I? and *How shall I live my life based on who I am,* are still primary questions. For black adolescents, however, the questions were specifically couched and answered in light of the realities of their race and class. These questions framed their quest for wisdom and were appended by the need to answer *What do I believe?*

The Civil Rights movement was a period of immense challenges to the self-identity, life direction, and beliefs of black people in general, and our youth in particular. Through what they did and what they sang, black youth in that movement showed evidence of religious ideological development. In the struggle for civil rights in both the North and South, youth fashioned a repertoire of values, beliefs, and attitudes about the church, the way God acts, and the continuing struggle for black liberation among black people.[8] In the South where the struggle was fiercest, says Shockley, "if it had not been for the leadership of men, women and youth, and students, the majority of whom were members of the black churches, there would not have been a movement."[9] I would argue that it was the sociohistorical events of the Civil Rights movement that provided the context for spiritual and political development of black youth.

Shockley's emphasis on the black liberation struggle and the involvement of youth forms the transitional bridge to discuss Christian hope in Shockley's work. Shockley concludes his chapter on "Historical Perspectives" in *Working with Black Youth* by highlighting new approaches to black youth ministry. He indicates that the "spirit of creativity" will guide new approaches that emphasize the particular needs and experiences of black youth.[10]

Pointing to the role of black liberation theology, Shockley situates Christian hope within a theological discourse about God and black people. He consistently challenges the church to center its educational ministry with youth from this perspective. In his essay "Ultimatum and Hope," Shockley asserts that the church is called to bring hope. This hope is specifically charged to European Americans whom Shockley challenges to join the crusade of the National Committee of Negro Churchmen.[11]

Discussion of Christian hope and black youth in the work of Grant Shockley demonstrates Shockley's own active embodiment of the Christian wisdom tradition. It also provides a foundation for the task of examining Christian hope in popular religious music in this chapter.

A Word About the Gospel Music Genre

Christian hope informed by the wisdom tradition of the black community appears in multitudes of art forms, including our poetry, plays, dance, and visual arts. It is also evident in the various musical art forms of soloists, choruses, and choirs from spirituals to hymns to anthems to gospel to rap to hip-hop. The genre of gospel music is also replete with variety. There is traditional, contemporary, and urban contemporary gospel as determined by the 20th Annual Gospel Music Excellence Awards given to professionals in the gospel music industry. Traditional gospel made its advent somewhere between the late 1920s and early 1930s with Charles Albert Tindley, reaching its peak of influence in the work of Thomas Dorsey during the1950s. Traditional gospel displayed through the music of Tindley has roots in the spirituals but also captures the "mood of disconsolation among the black urban population . . . [expressing] their own ethnic brand of hope, cheer, love, and pity. . . ."[12] Sanctified or Pentecostal churches willingly accepted this blues-influenced rhythmic musical art form.[13] Some of today's artists who are faithful to the style of traditional gospel are Chester Baldwin, Dorothy Norwood, and Shirley Caesar.

Contemporary gospel forms the second category of gospel that the 20th Annual Gospel Music Excellence Awards Academy recognizes. As mentioned above, this musical form was started in the mid-1970s and continues today in the work of many artists, including John P. Kee, Tramaine Hawkins, and, especially active during the late 1980s, Kirk Franklin. Franklin's work with his group The

Family demonstrates the complex nature of contemporary gospel harmony.[14]

Franklin's work exemplifies the last category of gospel: urban contemporary. Although Franklin vacillates between contemporary and urban contemporary gospel, his CD *God's Property* from Kirk Franklin's Nu Nation, released in 1997, signaled his ability to cross music genre boundaries. This youngest art form in the gospel music genre evolved during the late 1980s as a form of rap music, which is spoken nonintoned . . . poetry or quasipoetic narrative . . . delivered in a highly rhythmized fashion," and called gospel rap.[15] In 1989 Jon Michael Spencer defined gospel rap as "a form of Christian hip-hop . . . that speaks in the language of the black inner-city youth."[16] A distinctive marker of gospel rap, Spencer continues, is that it jettisons the white Jesus in the "old-style" gospel and makes prominent a black Jesus of the inner-city.[17] Distinguishing characteristics of urban contemporary gospel, also called hip-hop gospel and holy hip-hop, include poetic devices of religious songs (such as rhyme and figurative language, as commonly used in hip-hop) combined with a musical score and lyrics that invite—no, insist on—dancing. Also, hip-hop gospel is usually performed by young people of the post–Civil-Rights-movement generation or younger who dance, rap, and sing. The debut of gospel rap included artists such as Preacher in Disguise (PID) and MC Hammer.[18]

In what follows, I will explore four hip-hop gospels for theological evidence of Christian hope. They are Kirk Franklin's "Stomp" (Remix) and "My Life Is in Your Hands," and Mary Mary's "Shackles" and "Can't Give Up Now." Franklin represents the innovator of hip-hop gospel, and Mary Mary a more recent artist writing and performing in the genre today. There are many performers whom I could highlight, including Yolanda Adams, Kurt Carr, and Natalie Wilson. I have chosen Kirk Franklin and Mary Mary mainly because their lyrics were readily available.

Christian Hope in Hip-hop Gospel

It is impossible to explore the role of hip-hop in the black wisdom tradition and hip-hop's contribution to black youths' wisdom formation without considering the composers themselves, because their sojourns, as much as their music, are testaments to hope. Both sojourn and song reveal the black hope-centered wisdom tradition from which contemporary black youth's wisdom can draw.

Hope in the Hip-hop Gospel of Kirk Franklin

Kirk Franklin combines contemporary hip-hop music with contemporary gospel choir arrangements. Born of poor teenage parents in Fort Worth, Texas, Franklin was abandoned at age three and was subsequently adopted by his sixty-four-year-old aunt Gertrude. Although poverty and the problems of urban life posed many challenges for Gertrude, her vision for young Franklin propelled her efforts and creative ingenuity. When Franklin started playing the piano at age four, Gertrude collected cans to pay for his music lessons. On Sunday mornings Gertrude made sure that Franklin attended church. At age five, Franklin was singing and playing in various churches in the Fort Worth gospel circuit. At age eleven, he was appointed minister of music at a church. This professional position launched his career in writing and arranging Christian music. Gertrude modeled Christian hope, envisioned young Franklin's future, and acted in her own life and Franklin's with confidence. Even in the midst of hardship and poverty Gertrude persisted with hope.[19]

Gertrude and Franklin's life story, sketchy as it is, testifies to Christian wisdom formation. He learned from his aunt and the church the values of tenacity, hard work, creative use of resources, and vision; and he fashioned his talents into a vocation in the context of the Christian church. I would posit that Christian hope in Kirk Franklin's hip-hop gospel music is influenced by the wisdom tradition in which he was nurtured.

Franklin's "Stomp" (Remix) gave black worshipers permission to dance even in more formal black congregations where hymns and anthems are customary. Aired on radio and television's music video, "Stomp" (Remix) moved to the eleven o'clock hour of Sunday mornings when choirs led the congregation in "Stomp" and invited members to move into the aisles to dance. In the remix track, Franklin invites the thoughts of those who think that the music is too radical with an introductory praise shout of "Glory! Glory!" Franklin's words of introduction are followed by his reminiscing hard times that pulled him down into despair. His petition to Jesus is miraculous and brings him up from his down-and-out state. He sings:

> When I think about your goodness it makes me wanna stomp.
> Makes me clap my hands, makes me wanna dance and stomp.[20]

This hip-hop gospel proclaims victory over trials and troubles, depression and despair. It acknowledges these afflictions and quickly moves to praising God in word and dance, avoiding prolonged lament. It is the amazing love of Jesus that pulls the author up from the miry bog of despair and pain, planting him/her on solid ground for the act of praising God through dance. "Stomp" (Remix) implicitly resources Psalm 150:4-6— "Praise [God] with tambourine and dance. . . . Praise the Lord"— to exemplify concretely how to praise God. Praise is the antidote for difficulty, depression, and hopelessness. Franklin also uses call and response throughout his performance of the song by seeking from the choir response to the question "Can I get a witness?" And he testifies to "having church," which is his way of acknowledging lively, spirit-filled worship. New York rap star from Salt-n-Pepa Cheryl James (Salt) closes the remix with prose of praise to God.[21]

With rap lyrics, Cheryl James acknowledges God's grace that "brought [her] through" hard times. James borrows the phrase "brought me through" from the traditional vernacular of the black community that expresses a power far greater than one's self or any other human being. Again, praise is the indicator of hope, sending the message that in the midst of despair we are to praise God. Praise brings hope.

Franklin's second track, "My Life Is in Your Hands" depicts hope in more explicit language than "Stomp" (Remix):

> Oh, I know that I can make it;
> I know that I can stand.[22]

Here again hopelessness from worry, fear, and troubles is overcome by realizing that one's destiny is in the hands of Jesus. Hope is restored. Unlike "Stomp" (Remix), this song has a slower tempo, but it still invites dancing. The song is also both conversational and self-meditative in its move from a declaration to others not to worry (based on the belief that there is a friend in Jesus) to the self's claim ("I know that I can make it"), followed by the self's talk with Jesus ("My life is in your hands"). By assuaging worry and fear in this way, the choir gives its listeners reasons for hope and "teaches" a language of hope. The song draws from the black wisdom tradition by giving to listeners the very phrase "Joy comes in the morning," which caring mothers or revered church stewards have repeated from Psalms 30:5b KJV: "Weeping may endure for a night, but joy cometh in the morning."

Another proverb, "Troubles don't last always," captures the parent's testimony to a child or an other-mother's declaration to a young girl that God can transform anything and anybody.[23] Although this phrase does not correlate directly with Scripture, the assurance that trouble is finite and not eternal is still rooted in the black American biblical hermeneutic found in other passages such as "The LORD is a stronghold for the oppressed, a stronghold in times of trouble" (Psalm 9:9). The point here is that the phrases "Joy comes in the morning" and "Troubles don't last always" draw on both biblical and cultural wisdom to proclaim hope in the face of worry and fear.

Hope in the Hip-hop Gospel of Mary Mary

"Joyful noise," "dance-floor funk" and "as much fun on the dance floor as it is in the church" are three phrases used by the media to describe the hip-hop gospel sister duo called Mary Mary. Erica and Tina Atkins are singers/songwriters who define themselves as strictly gospel artists who reject the label of inspirational artists in order to give witness to their ministry of proclaiming the love of Jesus Christ.[24] These siblings, both in their twenties, chose to identify themselves as Mary Mary to honor Mary Magdalene, "who was delivered from evil spirits," and Mary, mother of Jesus, because both women were instrumental in Jesus' ministry.[25]

Erica and Tina Atkins were born to gospel-singing parents, who raised the singing duo along with Erica and Tina's five other sisters. Living in Inglewood, California, their mother and father strictly insisted that all seven children attend church regularly. They were allowed to play only religious music in the house. The Atkins children composed most of the church choir's soprano section, with Erica and Tina's vocal talents earning them recognition and leadership as soloists. The seven Atkins children made their television debut with the *Bobby Jones Gospel* program on the Black Entertainment Network. This decisive event encouraged Erica and Tina to pursue their vocation as gospel artists.

We can only speculate about the Christian nurture the Atkins parents gave Erica, Tina, and the other siblings. Parenting teenagers who grew up in the 1990s in Inglewood, California, was likely an act of fortitude and faith. Amidst an economic recession, inner-city violence and the Rodney King riots, parenting must have tested the spiritual tenacity of the entire family. The music of Erica and Tina bears witness to religious values they received in home and in church.

The song "Shackles (Praise)" is Mary Mary's first top 10 single. Like Kirk Franklin's "Stomp," "Shackles" blends the excitement of dancing with worship and praise. Also, as with Franklin, Mary Mary proclaims hope as praise to God. A guest rapper introduces the sound track of "Shackles" with, "O, it sure is hard out here, ya know; I don't mind though; I'm glad to be praising, ya know what I'm say'n?"[26] The rapper weaves call-and-response phrases throughout the vocal interchanges of Erica and Tina:

> Take the shackles off my feet so I can dance,
> I just wanna praise you, I just wanna praise you.[27]

Erica and Tina struggle against despair that holds them in bondage. Although hopelessness seems to overcome, they declare victory in God's power to break the chains of trouble. The word *shackled* is common in African American vernacular. The word invokes images of the black slave woman and man, bound against their will, moving with chained feet to the auction block. The message is that whether by chains or the bonds of tough struggles experienced in body, mind, and spirit, freedom is possible through the power of Jesus Christ. The first stanza of the William

Gaither song "He Touched Me," which is embraced by many in the African American community, also communicates this same feeling: "Then the hand of Jesus touched me / And now I am no longer the same."[28] Through lively prayer Mary Mary briefly borrows from the wisdom tradition to describe the state of hopelessness during hard times. Circumstances of poverty, violence, homelessness or inadequate housing, unjust incarceration, racial profiling, and drug-infested neighborhoods are "shackles" that render one hopeless. In the chorus of "Shackles," Erica and Tina request the removal of the despairing conditions of the metaphor and, through the request, affirm that God liberates us from the chains of despair even in the midst of horrific circumstances. Moreover, the chorus points to the act of praise to God as the means of alleviating the pain of conditions and events that bring on hopelessness.

Borrowing from the wisdom tradition, Erica and Tina sing a song of hope entitled "Can't Give Up Now," which reaches back to the heritage of the Negro spirituals. The original song is "I Don't Feel No Ways Tired." It was born in the slave experience but later arranged by H. T. Burleigh with a copyright in 1917. Burleigh indicates that the spiritual was based on Hebrews 11:14, 16. Starting with verse 13, the scripture makes reference to verses 8-12, which describe the faith of Abraham, and God's promise to make him the father of many descendants:

> All of these died in faith without having received the promises, but from a distance they saw and greeted them. They confessed that they were strangers and foreigners on the earth, for people who speak in this way make it clear that they are seeking a homeland. If they had been thinking of the land that they had left behind, they would have had opportunity to return. But as it is, they desire a better country, that is, a heavenly one. Therefore God is not ashamed to be called their God; indeed, he has prepared a city for them. (Hebrews 11:13-16)

The black slave community contextualized the above scripture based on their existential reality. Burleigh's arrangement of the scripturally inspired song describes the otherworldly home of heaven, for which the black slave hoped:[29]

I am seekin' for a city, Hallelujah . . . For a city into de Hebben,
Hallelu. . . . Lord, I don't feel noways tired Childaren! Oh, glory
Hallelujah![30]

A later gospel version of the spiritual eliminated the otherworldly language, but kept the refrain "I don't feel no ways tired."
The new lyrics declared:

I've been sick but God bro't me.
I don't believe that God would bring me this far just to leave
me."[31]

Mary Mary's 2000 rendering of the earlier versions holds the
redacted title of "Can't Give Up Now" and speaks the language
of the hip-hop community and others who were not weaned on
the gospel songs of the 1970s and 1980s. The 2000 version adds
new lyrics describing the existential situation of one who must
hope against hope. Sung in a slow swaying tempo, the sisters
sing:

I just can't give up now.
I've come too far from where I started from.[32]

Valleys of doom and battles of despair encroach on Mary Mary.
Yet these valleys hold the key to the singers' destiny even while
they question where their strength will come from. They
acknowledge difficult times as they recall how praising God lifts
them from the pit of hopelessness. The song's chorus is repeated
several times, changing progressively to higher keys to reflect the
mounting confidence in the words of hope that it confesses.
Ultimately, moving into an a capella rendition of the chorus, the
words "I just can't give up now . . ." are accompanied by march-
ing feet and clapping hands. With new lyrics and momentum, the
song "Can't Give Up Now" empowers listeners to move ahead in
the midst of obstacles and despair to aggressively seize hope
with the "blessed assurance" of God's grace. Erica and Tina's
lyrics build on, yet improve on the earlier versions of "I Don't
Feel No Ways Tired," giving the listener concrete ways of actual-
izing hope. The lyrics acknowledge the hardships and struggles
of life and offer the challenge and responsibility to stay in the bat-

tle. Regardless of victory or defeat, the decision to "fight" is critically important. The hip-hop generation—and, for that matter, others who hear the song—receive from Mary Mary the message that hardship and disappointment are to be expected; however, one can expect God to answer one's prayers for strength to overcome the hurdles in the race of life. Confidence in God's presence, despite loneliness and even rejection, is the final charge of Mary Mary.

The profound message of wisdom to black youth in Mary Mary's call to hope is that action in present-lived experience is needed as these youth make decisions about school, friends, work, leisure, and family. Hope is an action in the present world and not a passive anticipation of another world to come. In this way, Mary Mary's eschatology is consistent with black theology promoted by James Cone. "Black Theology has hope for this life. The appeal to the next life is a lack of Hope."[33] Hope is "a practical idea which deals with the reality of this world."[34] Cone's statements derive from his critique of otherworldly theology that predominates in theological discourse of the black church. Mary Mary's "Can't Give Up Now" counters this discourse and presents a new hope-centered wisdom paradigm with which the hip-hop generation resonates.

By far, "Can't Give Up Now" is a song of hope that speaks powerfully to black teenagers spinning down into the abyss of skepticism, cynicism, and despair. The song gives hope as well as challenges youth in the throws of choosing suicide or life, dropping out of school or graduating from high school, drug/alcohol addiction or a drug-free/alcohol-free life, overeating/anorexia or eating healthy. It raises hope and challenges youth to decide to celebrate their bodies as the temple of God, "a living sacrifice, holy and acceptable to God, which is your spiritual worship" (Romans 12:1), rather than engaging in sexual activity with its risk of HIV/AIDS and other sexually transmitted diseases. Identified as the song of the hip-hop generation of youth living in inner cities, Mary Mary's "Can't Give Up Now" has crossover appeal for mainstream culture as it encourages middle- and upper-class teenagers to hope in the midst of trouble.

Hip-hop Spirituality and Christian Spiritual Formation for Hope

The hip-hop gospel or "holy hip-hop" of Kirk Franklin and Mary Mary demonstrates some historical continuity of hope from the wisdom tradition of the black community. These musical artists link the past to the present through their continued emphasis on hope even though they affirm a "realized" hope as opposed to the otherworldly hope appearing in some spirituals and gospel music of the wisdom tradition. The value of the hope-centered wisdom that appears in their music lies in its "speaking" a language and story that black teens accept as their own. The hope-bearing message of the music has profound meaning for black youths' wisdom formation. Moreover, through affirming dancing as an expression of spirituality, hip-hop gospel has also given not simply black youth but the black community reason to reclaim the movement of our bodies in the church. These contributions of hip-hop gospel offer the black church an opportunity to create intentioned and relevant wisdom formation guidance of black youth in an age, to use Michael Dyson's words, where "there is a desperate need to reach young blacks, to touch them where they live."[35] This music holds promise as a center of critical conversation and reflection in the church's educational ministry efforts to respond to the very real search of black youth for help in surmounting life's issues and struggles. And the use of this music in worship promotes wisdom formation in ways that are empowering of body, mind, and spirit for both youth and the whole worshiping community.

There are two issues, however, that should be mentioned with regard to a guided process in wisdom formation using hip-hop gospel music. First, the questions must be raised: *When today's youth decide to "fight" the battles of life, what are the boundaries of their battles? Are their battles just for personal victory or for the good of all humanity as well?* If their concern to confront the forces of life that hold them down is strictly for self-enlightened interest, then this contradicts the wisdom tradition that promotes the value of community. The African proverb "I am because we are" means that personal existence is realized because the community exists. The historic prominence of this value of black people in Africa and in the Diaspora must be brought into conversation and reflection with educational ministry leaders and youth.[36]

Second, there is a need for more lamenting in hip-hop gospel before moving to praising God. Usually hip-hop culture briefly works out the pain of trial and tribulations using language of lament in one or two sentences. Using the psalms as a paradigm, guidance is needed that assists youth in hip-hop culture to develop this aspect of life so that denial of trouble does not take place and healing is promoted. Lamenting encourages healing and hope.[37]

Conclusion

In short, hip-hop gospel is a current-day musical genre through which black youth can internalize wisdom-forming themes or messages. This music exists as a resource for motivating, guiding, and empowering youth to act on values, beliefs, and practices that the black Christian wisdom tradition embodies. This wisdom tradition centers on living in hope and living after the example of Jesus, the exemplar of hope. At the same time, the thematic content of hip-hop raises an important caution for Christian educators who utilize this music as a wisdom-forming resource. Christian educators must consider and engage youth in conversations about the ability of hip-hop gospel to provide images that make possible their embrace of a communal ethic. Wisdom formation must necessarily emphasize being *in* and *for* community rather than accenting an individualistic orientation. Moreover, the use of hip-hop gospel in Christian education must include the concern for its ability to engage youth in honest and forthright experiences of lament that encourage healing and hope, in balance with praise.

CHAPTER 5

Counsel from Wise Others: Forming Wisdom Through Male Mentoring

Trunell D. Felder

*Wisdom is the principal thing; therefore get wisdom:
and with all thy getting get understanding.*
                                        —Proverbs 4:7 KJV

Wisdom is an endowment of God that we receive through our ongoing engagement in spiritual disciplines and participation in a faith community. We receive this wisdom through our discernment of God's will for our lives, and we show it through our commitment to carry out God's will, come what may. This kind of wisdom also follows our spiritual and personal transformation. The result of this change is our ongoing journey of being conformed to the image of Jesus Christ and of having the image of Christ formed in us.[1] As transformed beings, we experience ourselves as new creations in Christ. We intend to live the Christian lifestyle. Our goal is to positively have an impact on life in community. We *know* that we know that our strength comes from God, and we rely on God's guidance through Jesus Christ and the Holy Spirit in life's struggles that will surely come. We also seek counsel from wise others in the community of faith and offer direction that contributes communal wisdom. The black Christian church is challenged today to actively engage black males in this wisdom-forming process.

The challenge comes from an observation that, like the black family, the black Christian church has become increasingly matrifocal. For decades men have increasingly left the scene of mainline Christian churches. Far too many of our men have internalized the individualistic, competitive, productivity standard of majority culture that has engendered in them a counterfeit masculinity and their isolation from God, intimate relationships, and themselves. At the same time, the souls of these men have been scarred, oppressed, and in essence held captive as the result of the continuing evils of systemic racism.[2] Without a clear platform for wisdom formation, many black men have failed to gain the insights that would assist their embracing an alternative life-way and their confronting the realities of racism. Likewise, black men have failed to heed their deep yearning for spiritual development. In short, many black men remain spiritual infants who are disengaged from religious life and experiences with the Ultimate Source and human support of positive self identity, strength, and wholeness directedness needed for hopeful and constructive life in community. Far too many men falter in seeking God's guidance and in forming spiritual insights and common sense needed to address life's troubling, and all too often unjust, circumstances

It is true, of course, that black men acknowledge the reality of God; but their desire for wholeness and fulfillment that comes from an intimate relationship with God and fellow disciples is often not fully realized. The development and sustenance of this kind of relationship are central to black men's formation of wisdom. Thus, it is important for educational ministries in the black church to develop models for the spiritual and wisdom formation of black males that can assist and support this important relational dimension. In doing so, the black church empowers black males to nurture and disciple other males in the Christian faith. I present both spiritual and wisdom formation because I see them as having concomitant relationship.

There can be no wisdom formation apart from spiritual development. Both are the by-products of a blest and continuous relationship with God through Jesus Christ and with those in the human community. Jesus teaches us to love the Lord our God with all of our heart, soul, mind, and strength, and our neighbors as ourselves (Mark 12:30-31). Jesus offered these as the chief commandments, apart from which there can be no true development or formation of any kind. Therefore, wisdom formation is best achieved in an environment that fosters intimate relationships with God and other sojourners. In essence, the sojourners are involved in peer group mentoring relationships where they take responsibility for each other's growth and development. In this chapter, we will explore how peer group mentoring relationships can be undertaken. In this exploration, I will draw on my experiences as leader of a male mentoring program with never-married, married, divorced, and remarried black males between the ages of twenty-eight and sixty-five at the Ray of Hope Christian Church in Decatur, Georgia. Attention will be given to the nature of the mentoring group and the function of the mentor, followed by the presentation of specific characteristics and goals of a mentoring process involving black males.

The Nature of the Mentoring Group and Function of the Mentor

Male mentoring groups are a highly effective means of encouraging the formation of wisdom in black males. In fact, to mentor is to influence, whether with only two individuals or in a group. Peer mentoring that supports wisdom formation can occur wherever two or more individuals interact and influence one another's behavior.

In developing male mentoring groups, I gained much insight about the nature of the mentoring group from the work of Theodore Newcomb and Everett Wilson. In their book entitled *College Peer Groups*, Newcomb affirms that "groups have power over their members because two processes tend to occur together as group members continue to interact. Members become more favorable toward each other, and they come to adopt as their own certain group-shared attitudes, or norms, and to feel that those norms are right and proper."[3] The author is not advocating conformity. The important point concerns the adoption of shared attitudes and norms. Through an adoption of shared attitudes and norms, mentoring takes place.

Newcomb also identifies certain conditions that appear to be present for groups to influence their members. First, the size of the group influences the character of the participants. Newcomb writes that membership in very large populations is not likely, of itself, to bring about the strong interpersonal attitudes that affect peer group attitudes. Small groups are more apt to effect attitudinal change in contrast to large groups.[4]

A parallel can be drawn with a church population. For example, a church may seek to impress upon its whole membership through corporate worship Christian values and wisdom that will positively affect the members' attitudes for living. But small groups will more likely enhance the church's efforts. Sunday school classes, Bible study groups, and prayer groups are small clusters in which interpersonal relationships and Christian values can more easily develop. Likewise, male mentoring groups can promote these kinds of relationships. The point is that, in such groups, members are more readily influenced or mentored by group peers.

A second condition that strengthens the possibility of peer mentoring involves homogeneity of group members. According to Newcomb, "Homogeneity of age, sex, social class, or religious affiliation contributes to effective peer group influence primarily because of the homogeneity of attitudes that tends to go along with such similarities."[5] I have discovered that because of the homogeneity that was present in black male mentoring groups I led, the group members lent support to attitudes and actions that became indigenous to the group. For example, the common experiences of black males in the American social context, which these males readily disclosed in the group, fostered the group members' sense of cooperation, support of one another, and discovery of common values. Let me illustrate further.

In one of the group sessions, I asked the questions *What does it mean to be a man?* and *What makes the black man unique?* The group members concurred that there are positive traits of manhood such as being upright, leader, visionary, responsible, and self-aware. The men also agreed that to be a black male was a mixed bag of negatives and positives. It entailed living in our color of skin in a racially institutionalized culture begun in slavery perpetuated by Caucasians, harassed by law enforcement, having experienced social discrimination, and being labeled as lazy, violent, angry, oversexed, big, brawny, and stupid. But black maleness also embraces resiliency, adaptability, survivability, determination, and diversity. And the uniqueness and strength of black male character are found in his industriousness, creativity, responsibility, integrity, action orientation, tenacity, pride, sense of destiny, and teaching role. These positive characteristics that were disclosed in the group became important values that the group members strove to maintain. Moreover, the relatively small size of the group that made possible their learning and advancing the agenda together that these values are important to act on not simply within the group but outside the group as well. Over time, the group participants learned what was acceptable to the peer group. What became clear is that the mentoring group is a modeling group, where character traits and values are transmitted from one person to another.[6]

In an interview on his book *Effective Teaching and Mentoring*, Laurent A. Daloz told of the importance of the mentor by saying that "a mentor is someone who embodies our own dreams, who is doing what we hope someday ourselves to be doing."[7] Peer groups are a functional environment in which this type of mentoring can take place, because these groups create a space that exposes the protégé to the life and character of the mentor. I knew that, if the men were going to open up, then I would have to model it. Modeling meant that I had to surrender my own defenses before I could encourage their doing so. By giving myself permission to be a facilitator rather than *the* authority figure, I became a full participant in the formation process. My own willingness to be vulnerable not only modeled its necessity, but it also resulted in their allowing me the privilege and, in fact, inviting me to occupy their sacred space, the areas of their lives that they hold dear.[8]

Edward P. Wimberly also makes the point in *Relational Refugees* that "mentoring is a relational style of teaching. Mentors make themselves available to help students, congregants, and neighbors develop the skills for living in relationship."[9] The availability of the mentor is central to his or her being able to personally influence the development of another individual. Through availability, the mentor earns progressive access to influence the ones being mentored. In the male mentoring groups I led, I became aware that the spiritual and emotional lives of the men "were not avenues that had been frequently traveled by outsiders."[10] Under such circumstances, my availability had to entail my creating a "safe space" or trusting environment where they could experience the freedom and acceptance to share some of their most innermost thoughts.

As part of creating the safe space, I learned that the men yearned for genuine peer relationships. I focused on the reality that to be genuine means being transparent. I committed to being transparent with regard to my own life, the issues and spiritual hurdles I have faced, and how I have been able to "keep on keeping on." This show of availability enabled the men to shed their facades, to be who they were, and to embrace their potentials. It also opened the way for praying together, for encountering Christ together. And, particularly regarding wisdom formation, what happened in the group affirmed that the mentor must avail him or herself physically, emotionally, and spiritually in order to encourage change, for wisdom formation is more than a one-dimensional process.

Finally, in order for wisdom to be formed in black males, these males have to be exposed to other black men who are capable of transmitting godly wisdom that they have received. Though it is important for the one being mentored to identify with the mentor, in order for the protégé to mature in wisdom he must receive his identity from God. Consequently, the mentor functions as the guide to, not the source of, wisdom. The mentor actually serves as a model of wisdom and as a facilitator of the seeker's quest for wisdom.

The Mentoring Process

The purpose of mentoring black males is to guide their formation of wisdom. The wisdom to be formed in black males is their discernment of God's intent for their Christian witness in the world and their plan to carry out this intent in their everyday lives after the example of Jesus Christ. The wisdom-formation process calls for guidance of black males that results in their deepening relationship with God, self, others, and world. It is a wholeness-centered wisdom-formation process that both strengthens black males' relationship with God and effectively mentors them in ways that equip, inspire, and empower them to mentor others. In my own work with black males, three interconnected pairs of wisdom formation emphases held importance: (1) identity and self-definition, (2) transformation and relatedness, and (3) empowerment and liberation.

Identity and Self-definition

Historically, black men have been defined and their self-identity shaped by the dominant society in which they live. Black men have internalized the dominant sociopsychological images and expectations in society of what it means to become a man; and, at the same time, these men's positive self-definition has been hampered by the assaults to their blackness in racist society. Wisdom formation through male mentoring must surely focus on black males' development of a positive identity and on their becoming active agents in forging this identity in interaction with others and the environment.

Because the process of wisdom formation is analogous to a process of spiritual formation, the focus on developing a positive identity must center on who and Whose we are. In light of this emphasis, it is important that there is a biblical point of departure. From a biblical perspective, Genesis 1:26-27 connects both identity and self-definition in that it makes explicit reference to the *imago Dei*, or the divine endowment by which human beings are said to bear the image and likeness of God.[11] Taken from the writings of Augustine, the phrase *imago Dei* is traditionally used in theological anthropology to define the dignity and responsibility of human beings. The essence of humanity as *imago Dei* is an endowment of the Creator. Though impaired by sin, as a result of the Fall, the image of God is restored to its fullness by the grace of Christ. Thus, the restorative process can have much to do with revealing an identity that may have been hidden.

Though we are made in the image of God, there are many men who have not embraced that reality. Therefore, Genesis is the foundational scripture for informing us that our identity is established; we are made in God's image. To that end, self-definition is in part achieved from our identifying with our divine image, which is our identity. However, the reclamation of our identity can neither be done apart from a transformational process nor from our relatedness to God, self, others, and world.

Transformation and Relatedness

It has been my observation that many black males substitute activity (careers, recreation, civic, and other kinds of involvement) for spirituality that brings deeper and more lasting meaning. These men do not find in these activities the kind of satisfaction they desire. They yearn for a spirituality that goes beyond what the activities provide and for assistance to rise above the challenges of life. I have also discovered that, in so many instances, black males have difficulty forming and sustaining relationships with other men, and with their own sons, because they have not dealt with how the presence or absence of a father figure in their formative years has had an impact on their own lives. Black men experience much pain from their experiences of an emotionally withdrawn father or from fathers who were simply not there with or for them. Concomitantly, in their ongoing attempts to relate to one another, black men often choose vehicles in the form of sports, gangs, fraternities, and social and civic organizations, but they find in these activities superficial forms of relating. These vehicles fall short of producing the depth of intimacy that is promised and desired.[12]

The mentoring process that is directed toward wisdom formation invites black men in experiences through which they can discover, link with, and be transformed by God's presence and activity in their lives. Moreover, the wisdom-forming mentoring process engages black men in testimonials and experiences that allow their woundedness, anguish, and consciousness and disappointment of superficial relationships to surface, to be dealt with, and to be replaced by a new sense of who and Whose they are.

Transformation is inextricably bound to relatedness. Though one can claim his or her identity, transformation is key to self-actualization. David H. Kelsey states that "knowing properly depends on loving truly. I can know myself, and know God in knowing myself, only if I care enough to attend properly to God and myself. So to bear the image of God is freely to relate to oneself as a being in God. To cease to do that is to cease imaging God properly. Then the image is damaged."[13] Thus, transformation is changing to embrace the image of God, which cannot be done apart form divine and human relatedness.

I believe that it is God's intention for humanity to be conformed to God's image. According to the Scriptures, Jesus and the Father are one (John 10:30), of the same divine essence. Thus, Jesus as the human manifestation of God, models for humanity the image of God. That God intends for us to embrace God's image is seen in Romans 8:29: "For those whom he foreknew he also predestined to be conformed to the image of his Son."

The goal of wisdom formation is to engender black males' affection for God. But it is to be in a transforming relationship with God that results in their seeing themselves as God sees them. Moreover, the wisdom-forming mentoring processes are also to result in bringing about their transformed relationship with others.

Jesus said, "Love . . . God with all your heart, . . . soul, . . . and mind . . . and . . . you shall love your neighbor as yourself" (Matthew 22:37, 39). In that statement, he connects directly relating to God with relating to others; and he further suggests that loving others begins with the love of self. The important point here is that, in the face of black males' experiences of denigrating social and systemic pressure and, given the need for social and civic reformation and redress of this situation, the *imago Dei* can be claimed by black males when they rightly relate to God. Romans 12:2 implies that the ascension of one's consciousness to divine truth beyond world systems and stereotypes can happen only by a transformed mind. Luke Johnson, in his commentary on *The Writings of the New Testament*, said it aptly: "The gift of the Spirit empowers [one's] capacity to measure reality differently than by the measure of the world, and to discern in concrete circumstances the appropriate response by which God will be praised."[14] Wisdom-forming male mentoring processes promote black males' transforming relationship with God and their consciousness of the empowering gift of the Holy Spirit. But this kind of support requires experiences through which black men engage in honest communication about their past and present circumstances, articulate their need for and benefits of camaraderie, and envision a future undergirded by their knowing who and Whose they are.

Empowerment and Liberation

The relational difficulties of black males hinder their ability to grow spiritually and to act in constructive ways in their everyday lives. But when male-mentoring experiences address these difficulties in ways that foster positive self-definition and transformation, they feel empowered to take responsibility for initiating and nurturing genuine relationships. Certainly this kind of responsibility taking is important in the home, in the church, and in the community.

With particular regard for the home, I have discovered that black males have been exposed to a variety of models of familial leadership and they are often unsure how to function in that capacity. Dominant among these models is the problematic notion of godly manhood that is exercised through patriarchal supremacy and that results in a view of the "headship" of the man at the expense of the woman. The concepts of shared power and coexisting gender strength have been less than prevalent models in the church. My particular perspective is that spiritually strong black men who follow the teachings of Jesus are called to and capable of partnering with women and exercising leadership that will not oppress women in the home (and, for that matter, in church or community life).[15] Wisdom-forming male mentoring processes take seriously the need of black males to reflect critically upon their beliefs about familial leadership, on role models they are aware of and have undertaken, and on ways they may need to define or redefine their roles as family leaders.[16]

Black males also have vivid negative images of the role of men in the church that are based on past experiences and, in some cases, on rumors. As the result of the images, many black males have developed antipathy and apathy toward the church. These men identify the hypocrisy they observed in men whose Christian talk in church was inconsistent with their Christian walk outside the church. Some men recall tyrannical deacons who were a menace to the clergy. Still others cite the egotism of clergy and other men and the overall irrelevance of the church to men's daily journey. Wisdom-forming male mentoring processes take seriously the formation of practical steps to defining the church's functions and the nature of God's call to men to serve in the faith community. The processes intend to empower black men to revise prevailing perceptions of the church and how they and others behave.

An additional challenge pertains to how black males live the Christian faith in the larger community context in light of their seeming difficulty in identifying positive black male role models. In this regard, wisdom-forming mentoring processes extend the exploration of God's call to men to serve beyond the church in the community. The process aims to motivate and equip black males, spiritually, to become aware of God's intent for their lives and, practically, to recognize their gifts so that they may be constructive contributors and change agents in public life. This kind of wisdom formation emphasizes the development of a community ethic.[17]

Wisdom formation in black male-mentoring processes that takes seriously the above aspects is, by nature, liberation-oriented. This kind of formation recognizes that transformation or becoming a new being in Christ induces liberation. It is designed to free black males from what Anne Wimberly calls the "narrow boundaries of thought . . . and limited beliefs in the self's ability to act."[18] It is intended to bring about a fundamental shift in black males way of seeing life and being in life that frees and empowers them to act wisely in the home, church, and larger community, and world.[19] The desired result is that black males will grow to the point that they are able to be mentors who interact positively and influence the lives of others in these various spheres of everyday life to the end that others will, in turn, do likewise.

What I am proposing here is that wisdom-forming, male-mentoring processes are essentially and unapologetically focused on Christian discipleship. The processes take seriously Jesus' call to discipleship recorded in the Gospel of Matthew: "Go, therefore, and make disciples of all nations, baptizing them in the name of the Father and of the Son and of the Holy Spirit, and teaching them to obey everything that I have commanded you. And remember, I am with you always, to the end of the age" (Matthew 28:19-20). Disciple making is a dynamic and liberating process in that those who have been made disciples are commissioned to go and make other disciples. They are empowered by Jesus to have an impact on and transform the world in the name of the Father, and of the Son, and of the Holy Spirit.

Again, this empowerment is an endowment of God through the Holy Spirit who is able to guide both mentor and protégé away from non-Christian values found in secular culture.[20] For black men, to conform to the values of the culture is both limiting and debilitating. It will take a transformed perspective for these men to envision a reality that transcends the present and that empowers them to embrace future possibilities. It is God, through the Spirit, who will empower both the mentor and the protégé in this process.

Not only does God empower through the Spirit, but the Spirit also enables persons to act as liberating agents. In his inaugural address, Jesus said: "The Spirit of the Lord is upon me, because he has anointed me to bring good news to the poor. He has sent me to proclaim release to the captives and recovery of sight to the blind, to let the oppressed go free" (Luke 4:18).

Made in the image of God, black males are empowered for liberation. They show their spiritual and wisdom formation by becoming change agents in concrete situations. Their home, church, and communities are all potential sites of transformation and liberation. Consequently, wisdom formation must be about instilling values and emphasizing the importance of providing release for others. Jesus came to set the captives free; his disciples should do likewise.

Preparing for and Implementing a Wisdom-forming Mentoring Program for Black Males

In order for wisdom formation to occur in black males, the black church must be intentional in its preparation and implementation of educational ministries that include wisdom-formation initiatives. Churches prepare for wisdom-forming, male-mentoring initiatives as the result of their recognition of the need for them. Recognition of need derives from the churches' honest assessment of the nature and extent of black males' involvement in the life of the church, the situation of black males in everyday life, and the role of the church as proclaimer of the message of salvation and liberation. I also recommend that churches identify a core group of between four and seven men who will be mentored by a capable church leader through a mentoring process that will facilitate their wisdom formation and prepare them to mentor other males. Through this approach, churches move with intentionality into a males-mentoring-males model.

The core group may explore meanings of mentoring and functions of the mentor as means of developing understandings of effective wisdom-forming mentoring groups and their role in leading them. What I have shared in the foregoing sections may offer guidance to churches' entry in this kind of assessment process. But it is even more pivotal that the church leader who mentors the core group of men functions as a true mentor who facilitates their wisdom formation in the areas of identity and self-definition, transformation and relatedness, and empowerment and liberation. In what follows, I will present a three-part discipleship series, that includes a total of seven modules each of which is carried out in a one-hour weekly meeting.

Part One: Identity and Self-definition

In my leadership of male mentoring groups, I have presented two modules that address issues of identity and self-definition. The topic of the first module is "The Unique Black American Man." The session explores the exceptional characteristics of the black man. It is designed to involve the men in meaning-making and self-definition. It is particularly useful for black men because these men have been defined historically by external sources. Of course black men share commonalities with all humanity; however, when they are given the opportunity, they can discover innate traits or characteristics that are unique to them, and cultural wisdom that can contribute to their positive self-definition.

The Stated Objective: To explore our uniqueness as black men in American society.
Methods
- Identify key elements that make black American men unique.
- Explore perceptions of self.
- Determine how we can construct a positive self-image.

Key Concepts
- It is important to examine our social context to determine where we fit.
- Black men occupy a unique station in relation to white males, white females, black females, and other people of color.
- There is a theology and philosophy that we bring to situations that fortify our concept of self.

Scriptural References
- Psalm 139
- 2 Corinthians 5:17
- Ephesians 2:10

The second module is entitled "Faith of Our Fathers." The session presupposes that the role of a father greatly affects the social and spiritual development of males. A role model for the children, a father plays an integral part in building their self-image. The father models for the sons what it means to be a man. Furthermore, he indicates the importance of God to the life of a man. In this module, the men reflect on the relationships they had with their fathers. Through this reflection, the men share their stories and confront their very real feelings about the stories. Shared stories become a pathway to the men's formation of wisdom or insights about their past, the nature of relationships with father figures and with God, and about their self-definition.

The Stated Objective: To explore how the presence or absence of a father figure has influenced our perception of what it means to be a black man.

Methods
- Engage images of fatherhood.
- Explore how the absence of a father affects our self-image.
- Discuss how fathers form our identities.
- Suggest how to reform or transcend a negative paternal image.

Key Concepts
- There are various images of fatherhood that greatly affect our self-image.
- There is a need for the reinterpretation of paternal images in order for many black American men to acquire a healthy image of manhood.
- Manhood for the black American male must be redefined.

Scriptural References
- Genesis 1:26-27
- Proverbs 23:7

Part Two: Transformation and Relatedness

Two modules (modules 3 and 4 in the series) focus on the trans-formation and relatedness dimensions of wisdom formation in black male mentoring groups I have led. Module 3 focuses on "Black Male Spirituality." In it, we explore various ways black American men express and experience their spirituality. Based on the inadequacy of many activities to feed them spiritually, this module also gives attention to how men have related and can relate to God. Through testimonials and shared experiences, we explore challenges men have in expressing their spirituality, while also providing solutions to overcoming those challenges. Finally, through this module, men seek ways of engaging God at deepening levels.

The Stated Objective: To discover various ways of expressing black male spirituality.
Methods
- Assess black American males' approaches to spirituality.
- Explore how views of authority have an impact on a man's relationship with God.
- Discuss how the fear of the unknown affects spirituality.
- Discuss how the challenge to change affects one's spiritual experience and solutions to overcoming the challenges

Key Concepts
- For black American males, spirituality is an attempt to achieve transcendence.
- Because black American men have been the victims of oppression, a God that requires change and responsibility is often a challenge to male spirituality.
- Achievements, acquisitions, and addictions are attempts to discover God.

Scriptural References
- Deuteronomy 6:4
- Exodus 34:14

Module 4 is entitled "Developing Male Relationships." In order for men to enrich their spiritual and social lives, they must develop ability to form and sustain relationships with other men. Though every module presents an opportunity for men to relate to one another, in this particular instance the men are encouraged to evaluate their need for healthy male relationships and to discover ways of entering into these relationships.

The Stated Objective: To evoke a need for and develop an ethic for the care and camaraderie of male-to-male relationships.

Methods
- Reflect on the socialization of black American men.
- Explore how male bonding needs are met.
- Explore biblical models of male friends.

Key Concepts
- With regard to social interaction, black American men are socialized by both European and African relational standards.
- Because men need to relate with other men, we often gather around events in an attempt to fulfill that need.
- The heightened awareness of a need for male relationships may encourage men to seek positive and helpful male interactions.

Scriptural References
- Genesis 4:8-9
- Genesis 25:18-34
- 1 Samuel 18:1-4
- 2 Samuel 1:26

Part Three: Empowerment and Liberation

Part 3 includes three modules (modules 5, 6, and 7) in the series. The topic for module 5 is "Functioning in the Family." The module seeks to engage men in exploring how they may function with wisdom in their homes. Reflecting upon the effectiveness of previously observed role models and envisioning alternatives is considered to be helpful as the men seek to define their roles as leaders in the family. The wisdom toward which the module aims centers on men defining their roles as leaders in their families and arriving at a sense of confidence and direction in assuming these roles.

The Stated Objective: To discover how our faith can positively affect our functioning in the family.

Methods
- Identify various roles in the family.
- Explore egalitarian methods of leadership in the family.
- Develop functional roles that lead to familial empowerment.

Key Concepts
- There are systemic family roles that are indigenous to black people, which affect the way we function as black families.
- Slavery had and continues to have an impact on our family structure.
- There are social and economic systems that influence the health of the black family system.

Scriptural References
- Ephesians 5:21-33
- 1 Corinthians 7:1-7
- 1 Peter 3:1-7

Module 6 emphasizes "Men in the Life of the Church." The intent is to engage men in assessing how they have experienced the presence of men in the church. Assuming that the presence of men is important in church life, the men are challenged to construct practical ways of being participants in the faith community that can contribute to positive and empowering egalitarian relationships.

The Stated Objective: To construct a theology of male functioning in the life of the church.

Methods
- Explore definitions of the church.
- Explore male leadership in the church.
- Encourage male and female partnerships.
- Decide on practical approaches to forming partnerships in Christian discipleship as well as the cost and value of discipleship.

Key Concepts
- The church is a community in which men are a very important part.

- Men are called to leadership, not lordship, in the church.
- A shift from the patriarchal to the partnership paradigm will be key for ministry in the twenty-first century.
- In order for men to develop spiritually, they must be discipled by other men.

Scriptural References
- Acts 2:42-47
- Acts 6:3
- Ephesians 4:11
- 1 Corinthians 12:4-11
- Matthew 28:19-20
- Galatians 3:28, 29

The seventh and final module is entitled "Developing a Community Ethic." Module 7 engages black males in developing a practical plan for carrying out the Christian lifestyle in community. The intent of this approach to wisdom formation is for the men to acquire insights and skills needed to engage in a praxis-oriented spirituality or a spirituality of wisdom.

The Stated Objective: To construct a Christian ethic for affecting our community, defining our role, and evoking a desire to contribute positively to community and world.

Methods
- Identify problems that plague our community.
- Analyze the problems in light of our faith.
- Identify goals and solutions for addressing the problems.
- Construct a practical strategy for becoming men of hope.
- Engage in concrete acts of offering hope, including provoking the congregation to action through preaching, teaching, and coaching.

Key Concepts
- It is important to name our community issues before we diagnose and treat the problems.
- Because we believe that many of our social ills are physical manifestations of spiritual ailments, our solutions must be constructed as a result of our faith.
- In order to address our community issues, we must have and act on practical, achievable, and meaningful tasks.

Scriptural References
- Nehemiah 1
- Nehemiah 3
- 2 Chronicles 7:14

I contend that the type of sharing included here equips and empowers black males to engage and accompany others on their spiritual journey. I must emphasize, however, that the entire process is not a one-time experience. Wisdom-formation processes through male mentoring constitute a journey without a terminal destination. The men will find exceedingly helpful and, indeed, ask for the repeat of aspects of the process or even the entire process. I have discovered that black males have a yearning for an ongoing journey that will enrich their formation of wisdom and spiritual maturity.

CHAPTER 6

Conversations on Word and Deed: Forming Wisdom Through Female Mentoring

Anne E. Streaty Wimberly and Maisha I. Handy

Listen to advice and accept instruction, that you may gain wisdom for the future.
—Proverbs 19:20

Discovering wisdom to survive and thrive amidst crushing blows of racism, sexism, and class exploitation has defined the journey of black women since their arrival on the shores of America. This quest for wisdom and instances of satisfying it are documented in the work of a number of black womanist scholars, including Katie Cannon,[1] Emilie Townes,[2] N. Lynne Westfield,[3] Delores Williams,[4] and others found in a collection edited by Townes.[5] Indeed, wisdom needed for black females' growth, maturity, and resilience in the face of adversity has been passed on from one generation to the next by wisdom guides. These guides have been caring others and ofttimes provocateurs in intentionally formed Bible study groups, women's gatherings, workshops, and other hospitable gatherings in and beyond the church,[6] as well as in more implicit and casual circumstances.[7] Wisdom has sprung forth, says Dr. Townes, from "wives, partners, aunts, grandmothers, mothers, other mothers, comrades, worshipers, protesters, wisdom bearers, murderers, and saints in African American culture and society."[8]

Black females' need for wisdom persists in the third millennium, and their call for wisdom guides is rising amidst their craving for contact in an individualistic society that has disrupted the historical black communal or "village" functioning. In the preceding chapter, we discovered specific issues confronting black males that require attention and ways in which mentoring can contribute to black males' formation of wisdom. Our purpose in this chapter is to explore the role and nature of black female mentoring. The chapter is, in fact, our personal way of inviting the reader into a conversation on wisdom-forming mentoring kinships. We will reflect together on experiences of being mentored by females; and we will consider the wisdom we gleaned from them. Our intent is to discover the value of the mentor as wisdom guide, the church's responsibility in providing mentoring opportunities, and our own roles as mentors.

Toward Christian Womanist Mentoring

When we refer to female mentoring, we are really looking at two overall views of mentoring. In one view, female mentoring entails a structured process and intentioned facilitation. The second view is that female mentoring simply "happens."[9] However, we have observed that female mentoring actually takes place in both ways; and in both ways wisdom is often a powerful result.

In the Christian context, female mentoring has to do with a wisdom guide's imparting by word and deed Christian values, knowledge, and a vision of Christian living to the female wisdom seeker. The wisdom guide is the confidante who offers guidance, provides insights, gives feedback, maintains the integrity of the relationship, and models exemplary behavior and commitment to the spiritual growth and well-being of the wisdom seeker. But this role of the wisdom guide takes place in tandem with the receptivity and responsibility-taking of the wisdom seeker. Wisdom is received by the wisdom seeker as the seeker is open to it; and wisdom comes alive in the wisdom seeker's life when the seeker acts on it. Wisdom "happens" when the wisdom seeker lets the wisdom guide's message and modeling "speak" to her, touch her, and move her not simply to acknowledge her situation but to imagine what life can yet hold for her.[10]

Defining Womanist Mentoring

Womanist mentoring is the relationship of the wisdom guide with the wisdom seeker that centers on the distinctive journey of black females. This mentoring responds to black females' troubling experiences with race, gender, class, and oppression and issues occurring in their family, church, and local community life.[11] The goal of wisdom-oriented womanist mentoring is black females' formation of a strong self-image that transcends the sometimes mislabeled image of a domineering, castrating matriarch.[12] Moreover womanist mentoring is directed toward black females' consciousness of Jesus' co-suffering and empowerment of them to form and act on what Jacquelyn Grant calls "survival strategies in spite of the oppression of her race and sex in order to save her family and her people."[13]

Womanist mentoring is also concerned with helping female wisdom seekers form the kind of wisdom that guides socially necessary behavior (being strong), as well as an awareness of their finitude, need for healing (vulnerability), and requirement of self-care.[14] Moreover, womanist mentoring also pertains to the quality of relationship between the wisdom guide and the wisdom seeker that gives evidence of what N. Lynne Westfied calls "hospitality among dear sisters" with its embrace of intimacy, reciprocity, and safety.[15] In the hospitable relationship, the wisdom guide and the wisdom seeker create an environment of shared assumptions, articulated and experienced trust, and the giving and receiving of insights. What forms is a kind of hospitable kinship in which wisdom guides and wisdom seekers perceive themselves as being involved in what Anthony Gittins calls "a gift exchange" or the sharing of personality or "spiritual essence" of the self in ways that nourish renewal and growth.[16] In effect, this is sharing of God's hospitality.

The Importance of Conversation

Wise counsel has been passed on from one generation of black females to another through conversations of hope that exposed the stories of the difficult exigencies of life and despair on the one hand, and the means of "keeping on keeping on anyhow." These conversations draw black females into each other's company. Whether in formal or informal groups or one-to-one mentoring, the conversations function as opportunities to surface concerns that may not be welcome elsewhere. There is the expectation of mutual sharing and co-listening. Like the historical oral tradition of black culture, black females' engagement in conversation is typically narrative in form. Both the wisdom guide and the wisdom seeker share stories in order that the wisdom seekers' situation surfaces and the wisdom guide's insights, typically derived from experience, appear. The story of the wisdom seeker functions to organize and shape the conversation. The story of the wisdom guide serves to disclose new or alternative perspectives for the wisdom seeker to receive, assess, and decide on action.

The conversations and emergent wisdom of black females derive from the womanist quest for communal wholeness. Thus, narratives disclosed by black females also instruct and benefit not simply females, but black males as they strive for wise living. Black males also reflect on the role of black females' wisdom in their lives and reconstruct past paradigms. Although black females need healing spaces to converse among themselves, at certain times, black males need to be part of the conversations as black females strive toward wholeness. Whether in the company of females only or with both females and males, the shared narrative becomes the means by which wisdom seekers gain new insights into their lives and envision new or renewed direction.

Entering into Conversation

The conversations that follow are part of a group's dialogue on wisdom formation through female mentoring. The group met at Interdenominational Theological Center and was led by the writers of this chapter. It included black females and males, including seminarians and laypersons, married, divorced, and never married persons, and persons from the United States, Bermuda, and Ethiopia. The purpose of the conversation was to explore needed directions for black female mentoring in the third millennium, pedagogical issues connected to black female mentoring, and the black church's responsibility in promoting it. The kind of conversation in which we engaged suggests a relational approach for use in churches as means of guiding mentoring experiences. The group responded to these questions:

- What is the wisdom black females are searching for in the third millennium?
- What is the role of black females in helping one another form needed wisdom?
- How important are groups and one-to-one mentoring?
- What experiences of being mentored by females have made a difference in your gaining wisdom for your life journey?
- Is there a place for black males in the mentoring process of black females?
- What is the black church's responsibility for black female mentoring?

A number of key themes and issues emerged in the conversations. But the central one focused on the importance of re-villaging in the twenty-first century. The communal center of black life or the "village" is lost, but it is apparent that some of the village functions must be recovered if black women and black men are to thrive spiritually, relationally, and emotionally. Other themes and issues also surfaced, including one's dealing with single-parenthood, child-rearing, childlessness, and male responsibility; self-love and challenges in the lives of unmarried females; female-mutual-support issues, and negotiating the tension between communal versus individualistic value orientation; concerns for passing wisdom on to the young; the issue of trust and creating safe spaces for wisdom sharing; groups versus one-on-one mentoring; mentoring experiences in and beyond family in word and deed; and the role of black males in black female mentoring. The conversations revealed that developing positive self-worth and finding significant purposes for one's existence is related to recovering "village" functions.

Single Parenthood, Child-rearing, Childlessness, and Male Responsibility

Anne: What is the wisdom black women are searching for in the third millennium?

Adrienne: One of the main challenges today is how to raise the kind of child you would want to live next door to anyone, and to raise the child without fearing the government's interference in how you handle discipline.

Diane: Another issue has to do with being a single parent and how you raise a child without a father, and find support in that struggle. A lot of times single parents, especially women, are ostracized and looked down upon because they're not a two-parent household. So you need that support system, somebody you can talk to and say, "I'm struggling. What are you doing that makes it easier for you?"

Maisha: So it sounds like women are searching for more village consciousness. We do have different configurations, different definitions of family. There are some traditional definitions of family that no longer exist. Really, the traditional definitions never existed for us as black people because we had the extended family. We always had an entire village raising a child. But things began to deteriorate, and it became difficult for women to raise children alone. So we need more wisdom about how we can foster a greater village consciousness.

Challenges in the Lives of Unmarried Females

Anne: Are there any challenges that are particular to unmarried black females for which they need wisdom?

Valerie: Whether single or married, we are still seeking wisdom on how to arrive at self-love, self-acceptance, and self-esteem. That is an issue regardless of educational level or economic status.

Lovie: I think one challenge we have and may need to accept as single females is that we may not get married. If you look at the statistics, there are more black females of marrying age than black males. We also know that the incarceration rate of black males is high. There is the situation of drugs, homosexuality—so many issues that are taking our black men out of the frame of marriage. So I think that single black women may need to accept the fact that they may not get married, unless they make some adjustments or possibly lower standards in certain areas.

Adrienne: But that presents a problem; because if you lower standards, will you really be happy?

Maisha: So the earlier comment about self-love comes into play here.

Adrienne: Absolutely.

Anne: Do you think there are any fears of dating and marriage that black women have today?

Maisha: If I'm not mistaken, right here in this region, the largest percentage of African Americans with HIV/AIDS infection are black women. But because HIV/AIDS is in the black community, it definitely is a concern in terms of sexual activity. You have to know your mate, who you're dating. Married women, too, need to know their mate, because a lot of women who are being infected are married women.

Diane: You know, the whole issue of abstinence is being raised. Well, we can say that single, unmarried women should abstain from sex. But the reality is that most will not. So there is the thing of teaching safe sex. We put it on the back shelf and act like sex and the desires we have do not exist. But they do exist. If we're going to acknowledge that they do exist, then we need wisdom to practice what we call safe sex. That means talking about the use of condoms and educating about safe sex. We need to educate our young girls and boys, too. Sure, it's necessary to say to them, "No, I don't want you to have sex before marriage; but if you do, this is what you have to do to protect yourself."

Margaret: Where I'm from in Bermuda, the population is small— sixty thousand people—and the HIV/AIDS rate is probably lower than anywhere in the world. But fear is real. It's not curable. I really think abstinence is the key. And, you know, it can be done. We can live celibate lives. It's like everything else, it's a choice. But do our black women consider it the wise choice?

Anne: That's a big question that we must continue to focus on along with the rest of the thoughts that have been shared here. I want to move on now, however, to another question. How should black women help one another to find needed wisdom?

Female Mutual Support Issues and Negotiating Tensions Between Communal and Individualistic Values

Diane: Women definitely need to be more supportive of one another. Women tend to tear down other women more than anything I know. For example, instead of saying to another woman, "You really look nice today," we'll say, "It looks like you're putting on a little extra weight." Or, you know, "You need to do something about your hair." We don't recognize that when we encourage and uplift one another, we also uplift ourselves.

Gemechis: From my perspective, as an Ethiopian, I see a tension where black women are in the middle of an African type of village dynamics versus Western individualism. So that tension, that polarity, poses a problem. You see, wherever we are, Africans can't live without a village mentality. We need to support each other. It is our heritage. But since society has drifted into individuality, we have fallen into many problems. We need more than ever to claim our original identification and come back to supporting each other and developing a group dynamic.

Anne: What, specifically, do we see as the role of black women for black women?

William: A lot of black women's experiences have been negative. The role of passing on wisdom has to do with how you, as an individual, have made it over and what you might say to others in that same situation that would help them to make it over. Unfortunately, as it was said before, we live in a society that values individualism, so that what you have accomplished and your self-worth are attached to something that is external. However, if we were to look at the African perspective, that we are all of value, then we would be able to see how important it is to bring someone else along with us. It is a way of countering the individualism and of moving toward the communalism that is so needed.

Concerns for Passing Wisdom on to the Young

Maisha: There's a requirement on a very basic level for black women to take time and responsibility for younger women—for teenagers and young girls. I have found that even in the church a lot of our young women are starving for attention because they are not getting it at home, or they're not getting enough of it. Many of us can step in and take that mentoring or parental role—where you have those young persons bring their report card to you, even though there's no blood relation. There are so many things that are pulling us in so many different directions and, because of it, a lot of black women are fragmented, particularly in terms of time. But we have to take time to mentor younger women as if they are our own children.

CeCe: Not only that. Thinking of what you were saying, we have to show our young girls, our daughters, our grandchildren how to give a compliment. We have to say, "You look pretty today." I know because of the way my daughter does my granddaughter's hair; people will say to her, "Oh, I like your hair. Your hair looks pretty." And so [my granddaughter] now says to me, "Oh, I like your hair." So you're instilling in them that giving compliments is okay.

The Issue of Trust and Creating Safe Spaces for Wisdom Sharing

Diane: Being able to trust each other is the big thing. And I think this is the reason why women don't support one another more than they do. A problem is created when somebody, through past experience, entrusted a woman with a secret and found out later that *that* secret was shared with somebody else. When that happens, the woman tends to go along in life saying, "Well, she did it to me, so I'm not going to trust you." So there's a tendency to hold whatever we have on the inside when, a lot of times, we just want to say, "Hey, somebody, I just want you to listen to me. I'm hurting and I need to share what I'm going through."

Lovie: The way I see it is that our role as mentors passing on wisdom to other women requires us to be transparent. This means we have to be willing to expose ourselves, even the negative parts of our life history, letting another know that we weren't always where we are now and that we had some trials and made mistakes. We've got to get real ourselves so that we can help someone else, and let them know, "I was in this or that situation, and God brought me out; and God can do the same for you."

Diane: But again, I think that because of things we've gone through, we're not so quick to expose ourselves to people. In this day and age, you can't expose yourself to any and everybody, because the same thing you tell about your life or the things you've done, and the way God brought you through them, guess what? Sometimes that can be turned back around and hurt you.

Valerie: That is so real. But we have to take the risk and do it anyway for the sake of others, or they will continue to repeat everything that we have done. I think we ought to be ready to think or say, "Take my life and try to hurt me with it if you want. It doesn't matter. I'm free. My life is covered." So we've got to get to the point and say, "Let's press on with what we know we've got to do for the sake of others."

Maisha: I want to say in response, as we talk about the role of black women, that we need to intentionally carve out spaces where women can speak together, be together, and share together. Creating a safe space is a process, just as attaining wisdom is a process. We have to be continually engaged and intentional in seeking wisdom but also in creating safe spaces, whether through women's Bible study, prayer group, or through some athletic activities.

CeCe: I think also, as women, we have to be observant because we do wear masks. We get up in the morning, we put makeup on, and we go to work. We may be looking at someone and fail to see that something's not quite right. The sister may come to work every day without someone knowing that she's a battered woman. So sometimes we just have to sit back and look. Last week a friend of mine walked into my office and, immediately, she picked up that something was wrong. I had lost a very dear friend while my husband and I were out of town. The message was on my answering machine when I returned. I was just taken aback. It was hard. My point is that my friend was observant. She said, "CeCe, are you okay?" It's like the story of Hannah in the Bible going to the Temple every year—everybody thinking Hannah was okay. But Hannah wasn't okay. Hannah prayed, but her lips weren't moving. Imagine what she was thinking: "Can't you see? I'm not carrying any babies. I don't have any diaper bags. I want a child." Hannah had a mask on.

Groups Versus One-on-One Mentoring

Anne: In light of our discussion, how important are groups versus one-on-one mentoring with black women? Does one or the other make a difference, or are both important?

Diane: I think it matters. Again, regardless what we say, there are some things that I'm not going to share in a group, I don't care if you are the holiest of the holies. But when I get outside the group, I'm going to say to you personally, "Let me tell you what I've been going through."

Maisha: I don't think that there has to be a polemic, an either-or situation. I think that it can be both-and. It just depends on the issue that you're addressing. Sure, it's healthy to have some hidden-ness in your character. Psychology and therapists have shown us that there have to be some things that belong to just you. It also takes a long time to establish group trust. I'm thinking of Parker Palmer's retreat with educators—a two-year retreat. You need that kind of sustained commitment and interaction in order to establish trust. On the other hand, I do think that groups are important in terms of exposing people to diversity. And that is one of the benefits of being in a group as opposed to being in a one-on-one situation with another person. We come to understand different hermeneutics and various perspectives by interacting with persons in a group.

Mentoring Experiences in and Beyond Family

Anne: Have you ever had an experience of being mentored by a woman that made a difference in your life?

CeCe: Mine is just very, very brief. When my husband started in the ministry, I didn't realize that the lady I'm going to tell you about was a mentor. When we were sent to a church, if I wanted to know something I knew I could always go to Ma Fisher because Ma Fisher, who was old enough to be my grandmother, would always say to me, "Well, baby, if it was me . . ." She never told me, "Look, this is what you gotta do." She gave a "for instance" for me to think about.

Diane: I'm thinking about my mom when I was first called into the ministry. Prior to that, my mom's belief was that women should be seen and not heard in the church. One day when we were on the front porch—that place where people gather—and we were talking about women in ministry and in the church. I said to my mom, "What if I said God had called me into the ministry, what would your response be?" Her mouth just fell open, and she said, "Really? Well, my Lord, what am I gonna do? I need to start praying now." But out of that my mom was so supportive of me. Everything I encountered I felt I could go to her, even if I wanted to laugh or cry. It was like she was always patting me and telling me that if God called you, you've got to stand on what God called you to do. And don't let nobody turn you around. My mom has gone on to be with the Lord, but even now, when I encounter negative experiences, I still remember and hear the resonance of her voice telling me to go on and "do what the Lord called you to do."

Melody: Well, I know that mentors don't have to be talking with us. Like in the office, one of my colleague's lifestyle and the things she does makes her a mentor. See, it's not always the things you say. It's the things you do, the way you carry yourself.

Anne: So wisdom is passed on by example?

Group: Yes!

Adrienne: I was just listening to the other stories and thinking that it really is about how you carry yourself. I remember one lady who became my mentor later on, but when it became official we didn't have that much time together. It was a female minister. She didn't let men intimidate her. She stood firm even when they and other women would talk about her. The women would say that she did this or that, and that she was too loud, but she didn't care; she would always be particular in her dress and the way she carried herself. When I got older and was called into the ministry, she shared with me what I might expect and how I might handle myself. When I took classes, she wanted to know why I chose them. She wanted to know about my support system. She never told me what to do. She left it out there for me to decide. So the way she lived her life and the way she shared with me helped me.

The Role of Black Males in Black Female Mentoring

Anne: Okay. I'm going to ask a question for response first from the women and then from the men. And the question is this: *Is there a place for black men in the mentoring process of black women?*

Adrienne: I have to admit that there's a place for black men to mentor black women. And I say that because my biggest mentor was my grandfather, who helped me understand my grandmother and my mother. He's the one who gave me wisdom when I was growing up. When I came home from college and I wondered why everyone had changed, he's the one who took the time to explain to me that I was the one who had changed, because I left a child and came back an adult and saw everyone in a different light. He was also the one who explained to me so much about my relationships with others in my family. So, my grandfather's mentoring helped me get wisdom I needed for my relationships with family members to grow.

Donnamae: I also feel there's a place for men. Oftentimes my mentor was my father. He would tell me like it is—just like it is. If something was bothering me or troubling me, often he would see it first, even before my mother would; maybe because everybody said that I was daddy's girl. I just leaned on him a lot. He's deceased now, but I still remember and imagine what he would say.

Lovie: For me, I think we have to have a balance. There are men and women who have wisdom we can learn from. So we have to look at it both ways.

CeCe: I think that everybody has been looking at it from a family perspective. But a male can be a mentor without being a member of your family. I reflect on a mentor, Mr. Johnson, who was my daughters' school teacher. Every morning, what did Mr. Johnson do? He preached about life to those kids. And, for some of them, that was the only wisdom they received. He told a story that, as a little boy, he was homeless, he ate out of garbage cans; but that did not deter him. He touched countless lives. On another note, my husband was substituting at a middle school last week, where there is a dress code. They were taking pictures. A little girl came dressed totally out of code. So my husband called a female teacher over and said, "Is she in code?" The female teacher said, "No." So the administrator called the girl's mother to come and get her so the girl could change clothes. My husband said that the girl was in two more classes he taught after she returned, and she rolled her eyes at him the whole time. But I said, "Later on, she'll appreciate what you did." Well, he went back two days later. The same girl couldn't wait to say "Hi" to him. That's a mentoring effect. He was saying to her, "I'm not going to allow you to degrade yourself." And she got what he was saying. So, yes, black males can be mentors to females at different stages in their lives.

Maisha: Along those same lines, I think black men are helpful because they know other black men. Particularly when women are dealing with relationships with men, men can give you some inside information about the "brothers" that you may not otherwise receive from other women. And sometimes women don't receive things well from other women about men because you think they have a hidden bias or their own perspective. But when you hear it from another man that this is how it is, then you tend to believe it. So they can definitely be helpful in mentoring women about relationships.

Gemechis: I believe men can play a big role in mentoring women. I'm thinking of the Bible story of Mordecai, who mentored Esther. A distinct and peculiar voice can come from men that cannot come from women, because of the nature of men. But the work of child-rearing throughout the ages has relied on the mentorship of women. Men have been mentored by women. So I think that even though males can become mentors of females, still females need female mentors and males need female mentors.

The Role of the Church in Promoting Female Mentoring

Anne: I'm going to ask one more question that is related to the churches' educational ministry and the churches' ministry in general. Is the church doing enough to foster the kind of wisdom-forming mentoring processes that we've been talking about here?

Donnamae: That really touched a nerve with me because I'm in charge of a mentoring program at my school, and I get a chance to assign and talk with the female and male mentors. What I've found is that most often the Christians seek opportunity to be mentors in the public domain because the opportunities found there are not available in the churches. They are seeking agencies where they can act out the wisdom of their Christian way of life.

Adrienne: I have to come out of my experience. I was blessed to grow up in a church where, when you turned eleven, you were assigned a mentor who walked with you through the membership class. In fact, I'm still close to the person I was assigned to. We could talk to the mentor about anything. It wasn't just about church things. It was about life. They were trained on how to mentor us. They also had experience because they had been mentored when they were children. Now it's like the kids are just there. There are no adults working with them.

Gemechis: I think there is a misconception in the churches about mentoring. The church seems to be in the business of monitoring rather than mentoring. Mentoring that shows the grace of God, the love of God, the forgiveness of God has been replaced by criticism and condemning that has created a big generational gap that the church is having trouble bridging.

Anne: If you could say something to the churches today, so that they would get on board and do what needs to be done to mentor black females, what would it be?

William: We need to start with the young and recognize the pain they're facing. We are dealing with a third-millennium generation that has more information coming at them and the lack of direction for dealing with it. The church must recognize its irrelevancy. And the church must go out into the highways and byways to mentor those who would not come near the church. The church must also live the life of Christ so our young can see it clearly.

Valerie: I would say, "Just do it!" The church system where I am now presents the opportunity for mentoring, but in terms of the membership answering the call, it's always the same few. So, yes, I know we don't have time. I know we're busy. But do it anyway. I know the need is to go home after work, cook dinner, and take care of household details, and sleep; and I know mentoring may put somebody in a vulnerable position, but do it anyway! We also have to prepare mentors to live in such a way that their lives are living witnesses of wisdom.

Maisha: I think that our churches must also help young people to mentor one another, because a lot of times they can receive correction and advice from their own peers better than they can from an older person. We have to be intentional about that through such things as assigning prayer partners or accountability partners. A friend of mine directs a rites of passage program outside the church. The youth are accountable to one another; and the entire group does not progress unless they are all together, so they have to mentor one another and correct one another's behavior. If there's someone who's out of line or a person who needs some humility, or some forgiveness, their peers will come and tell the person, "You need to check your humility; you need to check your forgiveness."

Anne: It sounds like the mentoring task we are set upon in the church has everything to do with rebuilding the village?

The Whole Group: Yes!

Anne: Perhaps the message is that we have a history of being the mentoring village where wisdom resides and is shared. We can and must choose to be the village again.

A Way Forward

We invite you, the reader, to reflect on the conversation by calling to mind where you entered it, what energized your thoughts, raised questions, evoked insights, or inspired ideas for action. We also invite you to consider the following ideas that came from the conversation in charting the course ahead on black female mentoring:

- Give priority to the wisdom that comes from extended and fictive (nonblood) family.
- Find surrogate sisters, aunties, mothers, and grandmothers when blood kin are not available.
- Find conversation partners who can help you examine critical issues of life, including sexuality, safe sex, and abstinence.
- Commit to building trust and confidentiality in small groups to foster a safe environment for conversation.
- Recognize and promote the role that men can play in mentoring women, and the role that women play in mentoring men.
- Encourage your church to organize small mentoring groups and identify persons capable of facilitating these groups where females can tell, retell, and listen to one another's stories.
- Be part of the promotion team that fosters a faith community

where females can bring different perspectives and frames of reference to their lives without fear of rejection.

- Learn and pass on to the next generation caring and nurturing skills for use in mentoring peers and others.
- Learn and commit to connecting with others despite the pushes and pulls of Western individualism.

CHAPTER 7

Wisdom Formation in Middle and Late Adulthood

Anne E. Streaty Wimberly and Edward P. Wimberly

It is a source of constant wonder how trees seem to take the measure of the climate and make of their existence a working paper on life. . . . Yet, they do. . . . It is a very fine art, this bending with the wind and keeping on. . . . Bend with the wind but do not release your hold. . . . Bend with the wind and keep on living.
—Howard Thurman[1]

We commonly expect Christian adults to move beyond being disciples or followers to being stewards or leaders[2] by virtue of our assumption that they have gained spiritual wisdom and insight in tending to the issues of life. However, it is likely the case, as the introduction suggests, that our movement across the adult years does not automatically endow us with the full measure of wisdom we need for our ongoing journey as black Christians. Indeed, Howard Thurman reminds us that, throughout our lives, we continue to seek to know the meaning of life and our place in it. As Christians, our quest is to discern God's intent for our unfolding lives and how we are to respond to that intent.[3]

The dominant questions giving focus to this chapter are *How may black adults continue to grow in wisdom as they move through the middle and later phases of life? And how may the black churches' educational ministry contribute to the process of wisdom formation?*

The perspective here is not only that wisdom formation is life long, but also that it differs qualitatively from that occurring prior to midlife. In this society, wisdom formation in the early adult years entails the development of life-orienting perspectives and the production of knowledge and skills needed to make one's place in the world. We become wise through the process of defining what it means to make our mark in the world or to accomplish "wise achievement" vocationally, in family life and through religious practice. The focus is "making it" in the adult external world. This orientation toward wise-ness applies to both black men and women, particularly in cases where women have careers and work outside the home.[4]

In middle and older adulthood, however, the focus shifts from the external world to the internal spiritual world where we must develop wisdom for facing the last half of life. Wisdom formation also shifts to building a life-orienting perspective that brings inner meaning as well as resolve and imagination of how to give more certainly of ourselves to the next generation.

Four primary concepts give focus to this chapter. The first concept is *wisdom*, which is understood as the presence of an overarching life-oriented and God-directed perspective that gives structure, meaning, and focus across the adult life stage. Winston Gooden draws on Daniel Levinson's work to call this life orientation a *life structure*.[5] The second concept is what Paul Ricoeur calls the *second naiveté*.[6] This concept refers to efforts by middle and older adults to discern how best to undergird their life orientation or life structure with faith in order to continue the aging process even amidst life's challenges. Such a concept recognizes our limitations and acknowledges the mystery in life. The third concept is what Erik Erickson calls *ego-integrity versus despair*. *Ego-integrity* refers to our success in developing a life-orienting structure in middle life that is sufficient for our finding meaning over the older adult years.[7] The final concept is *worship*. *Worship* is understood as a context and activity that exist as a crucible or "cooking pot" through which adults probe the contents of their stories to the end that they orient and reorient their lives in light of the ongoing Christian faith story.

We will begin by exploring in more detail life-structure formation as the central task in middle and older adulthood.

Life-structure Formation in the Process of Wisdom Formation

Life-structure formation is central to wisdom formation in middle and older adulthood. As stated above, wisdom takes on a fundamentally different quality in those stages. In the first half of life, the life structure is made up of adults' choices with regard to vocation, marriage or nonmarriage, and religion. The dominant thrust is productivity and accomplishment in the marketplace, while including other dimensions as well. Wisdom formation entails adults' development of bases for wise decisions in light of existing opportunities with respect to schooling, a mate, friends, job, church and lifestyle and, overall, on one's wise preparation for establishing oneself in the world.

This endeavor is essentially the same for both men and women, though some differences exist between women who establish careers outside home and those who choose homemaking. If the choice is homemaking by women or, in some cases, men, then the content of the life structure formation typically revolves primarily around the world within the home and its community as well as the world of growing children. Work beyond home extends the life-structure parameters in other directions. Of course the life structure for both married males and females expands in a different direction than that of single adults. Wisdom formation requires attention to wise choices regarding having and rearing children. In the expansion phase of marriage, both mothers and fathers search for wisdom on child-rearing.

Wisdom and the Search for Deeper Meaning

In middle adulthood, the life structure undergoes a new transition. The orientation is toward experiencing personal meaning and direction for the remaining half of life. By necessity, the life structure takes on a spiritual quality and calls forth a search for a new sort of wisdom.

The book *Soul Stories: African American Christian Education*, includes the story of Mary Johnson, who in midlife reached out to God for new direction. Mary had come to a point of feeling doomed. She felt that her life had "gone down the drain." She experienced a marked sense of deadened purpose and meaning in life, feelings of inadequacy, and disappointment in herself for not reaching out for the "more in life." The "more in life" to which Mary referred had to do with her taking fullest responsibility as a Christian to help others find their way in life. She and her husband had successfully reared their children to adulthood, but Mary insisted that life required more from her.

Mary found herself "pouring out to God" her predicament after her pastor invited the congregation to tell God what they intended to do in the coming new year. After that experience, Mary entered into daily prayer. Over the year, she experienced a renewed call to the teaching profession, enrolled in school, subsequently received teacher certification, and received a teaching position. Mary's words about her redirected life were, "Hopefully, I'm helping somebody. For me, that's what it's all about. . . . I found it's important not to give up on myself. Don't get me wrong. Life still is no bed of roses. But God gives us a new chance every day. As long as I have this chance, I have hope."[8] Mary's husband, Carl, also confronted a similar crisis of purpose over the course of his midlife years. In the throes of that crisis, he opted for early retirement from a position in the business sector, followed by his greater involvement in family life as well as preparation for and entry into prison ministry. More will be said about Carl later.

The story of Mary and Carl illustrates that wisdom formation is about how we envision and decide to live our unfolding lives. Moreover, their story shows that, for Christians, wisdom continues to form, even in midlife and beyond, as we proceed in orienting our life structure to God's purpose. Indeed, Mary's and Carl's story shows their embrace of a spiritual quality of the life structure that is inherently narrative oriented. Their wisdom formation centered on their honest appraisal of the past and their intentional connecting with the unfolding of God's story in a new way.

From a Christian perspective, the faith story is about a living hope that is connected with the unfolding purposes of God for our particular life circumstances. It is a purpose-driven story that is connected to a vocation that God assigns to us. Our purpose becomes less focused on what we have done in the past or what we have accumulated or achieved. Rather, our purpose shifts to service to others and to the world and the desire to forge some kind of legacy that will make a difference in the lives of others.

Wisdom and Trusting Life's Flow

Learning to trust the flow of life also seems to be a significant dimension in midlife and beyond. Prior to midlife, we tend to emphasize making our way in life based on our own agency. Midlife brings opportunity to learn to trust the unfolding of the dominant plot of our faith stories. Midlife adults often become more aware that there is a narrative dynamic undergirding the flow of life, and that trusting the unfolding of this dynamic makes life more fulfilling. Pearl Cleage, in her novel *I Wish I Had a Red Dress*, says that faith is learning to go with the flow.[9] The chief protagonist in the book reminds us that a successful resolution of the midlife transition entails our learning to trust the unfolding of life's drama more, even though she had not yet fully arrived at that point.

Her minister friend, Sister Judith, seems to have mastered trusting of the unfolding plot of life. In describing the quality of plot trusting, Sister Judith draws on the wisdom tradition of the Buddhists. She points out the Buddhist's belief that when everything is in turmoil, something new is about to be born.[10] The difficulty we find ourselves in is a brief distraction so that the new birth could have privacy. This wisdom is also part of black Christians' biblically oriented proverbial saying cited in chapter 4, which paraphrases a psalm: Weeping endures for a night, but joy comes in the morning (Psalm 30:5*b*).

Wisdom and Addressing Life's Ambiguities

Wisdom formation in middle and late adulthood involves developing a life structure that facilitates the balancing of opposites in life. The purpose is to enable us to address head-on life's ambiguities and tensions. An example is the resolution of tension between marketing values and nonmarketing values. Marketing values focus our attention on productivity that yield economic and material gain, whereas nonmarketing values are concerned with communal matters and the qualities of commitment, nurture, care, and self-sacrifice needed for family- and community-building, or "village-functioning."[11]

The earlier mentioned story of Carl is an example of one who spent the first half of life pursuing a corporate career. This career largely meant many geographic location changes in order to move up in the organization. But there came a time when Carl felt the need not to move anymore and, rather, to commit more time to building relationships with his wife and children. Therefore he began making lateral moves within the corporation that took the pressure off him to travel and move. Having saved wisely, his attitude shifted toward lessened concern to make more money. He felt he needed to make a contribution to his family emotionally as well as to others. He began volunteering, which sparked an avocational interest. Later, his avocational interest became his new vocation. He made a significant transition in midlife from corporate America to a service-oriented profession where he transferred his corporate skills and developed new ones to mentor others.

Reconciling marketing values with nonmarketing values is but one reality that happens during the maturing years. Often, confronting life's ambiguities and tensions also entails reassessing relational values and cross-generational ties. As more people are living longer, many people in midlife are being called to care for aging parents. Moreover, in recent years, increasing numbers of middle and older adults have had to assume the parenting role for grandchildren, great-grandchildren, or other minor relatives; and in some instances these caregivers also care for aging relatives. These middle and older adults forego personal needs and expectations even when their envisioned grandparenting role was to be more social and emotional rather than instrumental.[12]

Of course, in black life, we have traditionally recognized grandmothers in particular as "the guardian of the generations."[13] However, the increased number of grandparents as child caregivers, both male and female, results from rising incidences of parents with AIDS, other illnesses and death; and parental abandonment, abuse, divorce, incarceration, teen parenthood, and joblessness or underemployment. The resulting needs of grandparents are often so dire as to demand special attention for their search for wisdom. They search for how best to carry out their "intercessory hope" or their act of standing with and for the children in the parents' stead for the sake of the children's worthwhile present and future.[14] Black churches help to satisfy this quest of grandparents/great-grandparents through providing "mutual intercession" in the form of spiritual guidance, affirmation of their strengths, concrete information about available support services, and models of parenting.[15]

Wisdom Formation and the Language of Lament, Life Acceptance, and Forgiveness

A proverb of black people is "If you want to make God laugh, make plans."[16] In Cleage's novel *I Wish I Had a Red Dress,* this proverb is repeated by Sister Judith as she talks about life's precariousness. It resembles another old black American faith phrase: "We can plan, but God can unplan." The point of these folk sayings is that life has many problematic moments, for which we can hold God accountable. But we can also count on God to respond when those moments seem to dominate; and it is this counting on God that opens the way for the Christian's lament.

The earlier story of Mary Johnson included her statement that "life is no bed of roses." In Mary's continuing life story that is not included in *Soul Stories,* this statement was reaffirmed with the death of her mother, followed by her father's death, the serious illness of a daughter, and her own diagnosis of cancer. The wisdom Mary sought and managed to shape with the help of the church evolved from what may be called a "narrative leap of faith." It was the kind of wisdom which prompts people to rely on the primacy of the faith story in those experiences of loss of loved ones, health challenges, unanticipated crises, and other stresses and strains. In these cases, one aspect of wisdom formation is raising the theodicy question or engaging in critical reasoning about why God permits suffering as means of making sense or meaning of life. However, wisdom formation is also about our entering into plot logic. This logic is an unfolding narrative and participatory "reasoning" that centers on our waiting until the next scene and next chapter of life to open; and in our waiting, though we are suffering, we make a narrative leap of faith that compels us to say, "Nevertheless, I will trust God"; or as Job said, "I know that my redeemer lives" (Job 19:25a). Indeed, this narrative leap of faith is the expression of Christian wisdom or the kind of wise perspective of life on which positive life structure in midlife and later life depends.

The language of lament is a way of entering into conversations with God about why God permits suffering and about "how long, O God, how long?" Wisdom is hewn in the throes of the language of lament. Through this language we cry out about disappointing and even devastating relational realities, disturbing events in past and present life, aging- and health-related issues, other unexpected and new circumstances, and fears about the unknown future. Wisdom formation is about learning the language of lament, which really is about learning to take our complaints and the realities of life directly to God.

In the narrative genre of the Bible, lament almost always reveals a responsive God in people's times of challenge. Black Christians' awareness of the responsive God underlies the folk expressions "God will show up; and when God shows up, God will show out," and "God may not come when we want God, but God is right on time." Lament is complaining to God with the expectation that God has not forsaken us. This understanding has remained part of the life structure, especially of middle-aged and senior black Christians. Wisdom formation encompasses these adults' coming to new or renewed awareness of God's for-us-ness. Black churches are called to assist these persons' wisdom formation through providing times for testimony; explicating the importance, nature, and role of lament; disclosing and using lament found in Scripture; and inviting the lament during prayer periods and meetings.

A significant dimension of the life structure that is a corollary to lament is our acceptance of or "making peace" with our only life cycle. This is the primary task of Erikson's final life cycle stage, *ego integrity versus despair*. Wisdom formation happens as we move to the point of acknowledging and lamenting that we cannot go back and relive our lives. This wisdom formation is not resignation. Rather, it is an active "coming to grips" with the totality of our lives. Indeed, it might be said that the price of not "coming to grips" with the lives we have lived is despair.

The black church can contribute to this kind of wisdom formation especially through nurturing rituals carried out in worship services, Bible study and prayer meetings, church school classes, and other age-specific and intergenerational groups. Rituals provide spiritual and social supports, allow people to get in touch with their emotions and attitudes, and offer stories, information, and ideas facilitative of new patterns of thought, feelings, and behaviors. However, in cases where individuals experience severe emotional difficulty, wisdom formation that leads to life acceptance may need to be nurtured by pastoral care and counseling.

Another dimension of life acceptance regards our facing up to biological changes as we grow older. Part of black American mid- and later-adult wisdom is captured by the expressions "Senior memories are catching up with me," or "I can't move as fast as I once did," or "My get-up-and-go just got up and went." Wisdom formation is our shaping a mid- and later-life structure in which we accept our changing physical self, resolve to care for our bodies through proper attention to health care, and see ways to participate in the affairs of life to the extent that we are able. The churches' educational ministry role is to promote this kind of wisdom formation. By so doing, black churches contribute to our discoveries of life's possibilities, awareness of God's gift of mature life, and consciousness of the requirement to care for that gift.

Learning to lament and to accept the aging stage of the life cycle is also accompanied by our ability to forgive ourselves. Cleage refers to "going with the flow" as one's way of moving on in life as the result of learning to forgive oneself for not engaging fully in all the opportunities life presents. People in midlife and beyond sometimes say, "If I could just go back in time, I would do this or that differently." In this stage, we know that we have availed ourselves of some opportunities and denied some of the options that came our way; and we know that we have had both positive and negative relationships with others. Wisdom formation that leads us to a positive life structure results in our acceptance of ourselves despite some unfulfilled expectations of self.

At the same time, wisdom formation that centers on self-acceptance does not mean that we acquiesce to and continue to carry out irresponsible or hurtful behavior. Nor does it mean that we abdicate responsibility for seeking the restoration of damaged relationships with others whom we have hurt or who have hurt us. In our maturing years, our development of a wisdom-centered life structure must necessarily focus on our seeing ourselves as we really are and on our seeking opportunities to "set the record straight," by asking the forgiveness of others and forgiving others.

With particular reference to forgiveness in family relations, it is well to be aware that the search for wisdom can be complex and fraught with difficulty. Forgiveness may be neither easily accomplished nor realized in a one-time event. For example, a senior adult in her seventies experienced ongoing depression because of her memories of abusive treatment at the hands of her stepfather during her childhood and her lack of surety that her mother really loved her. Because both her stepfather and her mother were deceased, there was no opportunity for in-person resolution. The senior adult relied on sermons, songs, and prayers of worship for sustenance and encouragement; and sharing with peers who had similar experiences proved helpful. However, a close and trusted spiritual guide provided the greatest help in the senior adult's work of forgiveness and arrival at a place of self-acceptance. She came to a point of admitting that her deep emotional pain caused by her stepfather seemed to grow less over time. On one occasion of reflecting on the past, she also remembered a time as an adult when, during a visit, her mother embraced her and told her how much she loved her and how proud she was of her. What evolved from this reflection was this woman's affirming embrace of herself as well as her pronounced sensitivity to the importance of validating the worth of others.

Whatever the case may be, any work of forgiveness that is undertaken, to use Terry Hargrave's words, "is a trustworthy expression of faith and care to the intergenerational heritage and posterity of all people."[17] For this reason our churches must have an interest in people's forming wisdom that addresses matters of forgiveness. The needed role of black churches is to be the nurturer of wisdom formation. The church nurtures persons in midlife and later life especially through sermons, church school groups, Bible study and prayer groups, home-based experiences, and other stage-related and intergenerational educational ministry contexts about the importance and nature of the work of forgiveness. Nurture also includes guiding persons in raising and addressing questions about their moral responsibility in the face of claims of others.[18] Most important, churches must carry out the obligatory nurturing function of proclaiming ultimate divine forgiveness, following the teaching of Ephesians 4:32 and the Lord's Prayer.[19]

Worship, Celebration, and Wisdom Formation in Midlife and Latelife

We will begin here with a personal account of our own parents' particular journey into and through their senior adult years, which was punctuated by what we observed as the "call of worship." For our parents, every Sunday was what they called "the Holy day," or the Sabbath. On this day, as long as they were able, attending church was an absolute necessity because God invited their presence there and because, in that Holy place, they could commune with God in the fellowship of others. Even during times of physical challenge they would steadfastly inquire, "Are we going to church?" These special loved ones in our lives pressed toward the Sabbath worship, whenever able, and always seemed to emerge from it with new insight, resolve, and vigor, indeed renewed wisdom, that allowed them to "continue on the journey as long as life shall last," as one of our dads would say.

The "call of worship" on the Sabbath was typically extended by their daily experience of prayer and devotions at home. This approach to the "holy day" expanded to include televised or taped worship, brief times of praying, singing, and Bible reading with relatives and visiting "saints" when poor health precluded their attendance at church. During these times of worship beyond the church building, our parents created new avenues for their ongoing wisdom formation. Whatever the form, worship was what one of our mothers called the experience of "the all-wise God's welcome." She called worship the time to say without embarrassment, "God, you and I have to talk." For her, worship was wisdom-forming time that occasioned crying, singing, and celebrating what she referred to as "God's love that will not let us go and that will give us what we need in the midst of change, challenge, joy, frustration, and the shadow of death."

Worship has special meaning for black adults as they move toward and into the older years. Black church worship is the context for celebrating time already lived and anticipating time yet to be lived as well as discovering or rediscovering how best to live now. Worship is the mature Christian adults' continuing wisdom formation that focuses on what it means to live out the fullness of time. In what follows, we will say more about celebration in black worship as an instrument both of wisdom formation and wisdom confirmation during persons' aging process.

A View of Celebration in Black Worship

Celebration in the black worshiping congregation occurs through an emotional environment that is marked by joyful exuberance in response to the wisdom that comes from God.[20] This environment is hallowed space where God's wisdom is mediated through "an oratory of hope"[21] carried out in sermon, song, prayer, and through signs of promise shown in symbols such as the cross and gestures like laying on of hands. Especially through these means, senior adult worshipers connect with the divine presence; and they gain, as the hymn says, "wisdom for the facing of this hour" and "wisdom for the living of these days" ("God of Grace and God of Glory"). These channels of God's wisdom evoke senior adult worshipers' formation of wisdom that they need to navigate their distinctive terrain of life.

Black congregational worship is also an occasion for senior adults' wisdom-giving testimonies. Indeed, a gift of senior adults in the worshiping congregation is their bearing witness to how they have journeyed through the experiences of life, thereby providing awareness, insights, and spiritual rootedness needed by the young.[22]

Celebratory worship signifies the worshipers' significant relationship to God and to other people. Celebration emerges spontaneously as wisdom is born *in* us and confirmed through the quality of emotional connectedness or relatedness *between* us, God, and others. The important point is that wisdom formation takes place *within* us, but it is hewn *in relationship* with God and others. A wise understanding of the significance of who we are in community and whose we are in God is borne out of community and confirmed in celebration.

Celebration, Rites of Passage, and Wisdom Formation

Celebration in black churches is connected to rites of passage. Rites of passage are community ceremonies that accompany predictable and unpredictable changes and transitions in the lives of people from birth to death.[23] There are rites for separation and for funerals, rites of incorporation such as marriage, and rites of transition for pregnancy, marriage, and initiation. In the later stages of the life cycle, rites of passage are related to older-life transitions such as retirement, the observances of twenty-fifth and fiftieth wedding anniversaries, late-life birthdays, and longevity in congregational life. The church's provision of later-life transitions is of particular importance here because of the significance of these rites in confirming wisdom already acquired and in pointing to wisdom yet needed.

Celebrations of rites of passage, particularly in middle and later years, are occasions for wisdom confirmation. For example, the recognition of couples whose marriages are longstanding and the formal celebration of rites of passage for couples celebrating twenty-five and fifty or more years of marriage gives opportunity for disclosure and confirmation of wisdom. The celebration of longevity and wisdom found in values, attitudes, and approaches to marriage honor the couples and provide inspiration to others.

The kind of inspiration to which we are referring is found in the words of Ruby Dee and Ossie Davis, noted thespians whose marriage of nearly fifty years is highlighted in Steven Barboza's book *The African American Book of Values*. Ruby Dee tells how important it is for couples who have been together for a long time to have opportunity to talk about it. She says, "We must talk about it. We are older, we have to say things, we have to hand down messages. We have to *be* elders because the tribe needs its elders."[24] The wisdom of Ossie Davis is highlighted in his words about the marital relationship that moved from "love, passion, blind sex, fulfillment and the joy of all the physical aspects of it . . . [to] the true objective of marriage . . . [when] you become partners, working together and appreciating each other as creative and productive people. And finally, if you're smart and lucky and wise, you end up friends."[25]

Celebrations of individuals' rites of passage to retirement, senior-adult birthdays, and longevity in congregational life are opportunities to recognize individuals' contributions to community and to emphasize the wisdom they can pass to the next generation. These celebrations create an opening for posing the question, *Is there not something of the wisdom of senior adults that can help us?*

Indeed, of critical importance in the ritual and celebratory life of the faith community is the role of senior adults as bards or poets who know and can tell the community's story.[26] Wisdom formation in middle and senior adults relates to developing a life structure that can sustain their sense of emotional, relational, and spiritual integrity as they continue through the life cycle. Undergirding these celebrations is not simply recognition of lived life but of recognizing the need for ongoing wisdom that can assure ego-integrity and the development of a life structure that brings life meaning in the face of finitude and death.

A Challenge to the Church's Response in Support of Midlife and Latelife Wisdom Formation

Black churches face a challenge today that has the potential for short-circuiting the wisdom formation of middle and older adults. This challenge regards the style of worship. Many of these adults who have long histories of worship participation have become accustomed to particular approaches to worship and styles of music. Moreover, they hold to familiar characteristics of worship because they have received wisdom and continuing nurture from relative consistency in the character of worship.

It is often difficult for adults in midlife and latelife to adapt to new styles and expressive mannerisms that are designed to appeal to the young. However, these adults desire to be connected with younger generations and are open to divergent worship styles so long as there is opportunity for them to be afforded some experiences in their own accustomed ways of worshiping. What are churches to do? We want to suggest here that it is important for churches to sensitively respond to the worship needs of all worshipers, including those in midlife and latelife. This kind of sensitivity is best carried out by including various genres of music and approaches to worship within a given worship service or through a system of alternation.

We are aware of churches where Sunday worship services are alive with creative responses to all ages. Young and old alike join in singing spirituals and hymns, teens offer liturgical dance, family units read the Scripture, young adult song leaders guide the singing of praise songs, middle and older adults pray, and the intergenerational choir maintains a wide repertoire of music. In one instance, a congregation held an intergenerational forum during which the young successfully taught the adults rap music and the eldest among them taught the young successfully the historical black musical style of lining a hymn.

Over the years, worship and especially the music within it, has nourished black people, soothed their hurts, and given wise instruction for an ofttimes difficult journey. Worship has been a powerful teacher of black cultural perspectives on Christian faith and life. Through worship, black people have discovered and passed on to others a spirituality of wisdom that encompasses a way of being disciples of Jesus Christ. The challenge to black churches is to assure that this historical function continues for every age and stage within them.

A Concluding Word

We have proposed here that the midlife and later-life structure is an orienting perspective that informs how we live the second half of our lives. It is made up of folk wisdom growing out of experience and interaction with the narratives of the faith. Narrative wisdom shapes a life structure that facilitates "going with the flow of life" and trusting in God's for-us-ness. Narrative wisdom also makes possible our experience of the second naiveté in which we recognize the limitations of life and the faith story, but we give our lives over to it anyway. The midlife and later-life structure is a buffer against despair in that we are able to forgive ourselves, accept our life cycle, and continue on in life until death. Finally, worship as celebratory experience and celebrations of long marital relationships, rites of passage to retirement, late-life birthdays, and longevity of congregational life are means of confirming wisdom already acquired and of promoting ongoing wisdom formation. Through these celebrations, black adults in middle and late adulthood develop a life structure that is hopeful.

CHAPTER 8

The Formation of Wisdom
and Human Sexuality

Edward P. Wimberly

I need wisdom. The quality that will make clear to me the significance, the relatedness of things that are a part of my daily experience—this I lack again and again. I need wisdom to cast a slow and steady radiance over all my landscape in order that things, choices, deeds may be seen in their true light—the light of the eternal and the timeless.

—Howard Thurman[1]

We are living in a critical period in the history of the black community and church. It is a time when much is being said about human sexuality and sexual morality from adolescence through adulthood. Yet it is also a time when much confusion exists regarding what human sexuality and sexual morality mean and how to address them. In the midst of this consternation, we believe that religion is the backbone of the black community and that religion and religious leaders should have a shaping influence on attitudes and behaviors concerning sexuality and sexual practices. Our churches, their educational ministries, and the leaders responsible for them are important points of reference and guides of wisdom formation that embrace the development of values, attitudes, maturity, and skills needed to be sexually healthy.[2] The question may be rightly asked, *What is the nature of wisdom the churches must provide regarding sexuality and sexual behaviors in an age of conflicting views and at a time when the incidence of HIV/AIDS and sexually transmitted diseases (STDs) in the black community continues to rise?*

Let me begin by saying that there is a wisdom tradition with regard to black sexuality, and it includes African naturalism, Greco-Roman Christian sexual orthodoxy, and racial-sexual stereotypes. For example, black people in America have been known to embrace their bodies, while at the same time being very suspicious of the power of the sexual drive. In addition, racism has forced these people to be conflicted about affirming their sexual desires or African background because of racist sexual stereotypes. Moreover, several levels of conversations about sexuality take place in black churches. These levels include public pronouncements and doctrinal statements as well as behavioral activity taking place in churches. At the doctrinal level, black people remain theologically conservative, meaning that sexual intercourse must be confined to heterosexual marital relationships.[3] At the behavioral level, however, a diversity of sexual practices exist that are tolerated depending on the congregation and the denomination. Sexual-oriented conversations among young contemporary blacks abound, and include open talk about contraception, AIDS, sexual practices, sexual pleasuring, sexual additions, sexual dysfunctioning, sexual desire and fantasies, extramarital affairs, homosexuality, and domestic violence.[4] Moreover, given the abundance of interest in sexuality issues within black Christian circles, formation of wisdom in human sexuality matters is a compelling topic.

Two specific questions will dominate this chapter. The first question is, *What are the sources and nature of wisdom with regard to human sexuality within the black Christian community?* The second question is, *How may the black churches' educational ministry serve as a wisdom guide in addressing particularly HIV/AIDS and sex education?*

Sources and Nature of Sexual Wisdom

Black Christians draw from several sources of wisdom with regard to human sexuality. One source comes from our faith tradition, and it includes normative texts and church doctrinal pronouncements or tradition. A second source includes the developments in science that are grounded in research of human sexuality. The third source is human experience and how human reason is used to derive wisdom from experience. The key is that in our contemporary culture, all three of these sources interact to help people come to some understanding of human sexuality.

The concern for the normative dimension is related to how these three different sources interact to form wisdom. The normative dimension has to do with what ought to be the norms or standards governing people's sexual attitudes and sexual behavior. Answers to the normative question vary depending on the starting point that one takes with regard to the sources. For example, should the starting point be Scripture and tradition, science, or experience?

The Social Construction of Sexuality

From the standpoint of the social construction of sexuality, important attention needs to be given to anthropological studies that cut across cultures. From a cross-cultural perspective of human sexuality, each culture has its own indigenous configuration that informs sexual behavior and assumptions about sexuality.[5] Sociologists like Peter Berger and Thomas Luckmann focus on the reality that all of our understandings of sexuality are socially located and that all of our understandings about sexuality are socially constructed rather than existing as a fixed biological reality.[6] Thus, biological dimensions of sexuality and what is considered to be normative are socially constructed.

Several principles help clarify the meaning of the social construction of sexuality. The first is that the physical and biological development of a person always takes place within a social environment. Second, human beings are open systems so that there is an open exchange between our biological selves and social surroundings. Third, our instinctual structure is characterized by plasticity in the sense that it does not interact or develop in a fixed way. It is pliable. The point is that our understanding of sexual desire, sexual expression, and gender-related concerns is very complex, and the meaning that sexuality has for us is socially constructed.

The way we construct our understandings of sexuality also has a history.[7] There is no way to extricate biological sexual drives and sexual expression from social meanings. Therefore, Scripture, tradition, experience, and reason are critical in determining what kind of wisdom about sexuality is to be communicated. The key is

142

that each local congregation must enable its congregants at all levels to explore the meaning of human sexuality drawing on a variety of sources, including Scripture, tradition, experience, and reason. Some congregations and denominations will come down differently on what is normative about understanding human sexuality. The focus here is on the process of developing human wisdom about sexuality and how it gets communicated across generations.

Diverse Approaches to Understanding Sexuality

There are diverse approaches to sexuality with black congregations and denominations. The goal in describing the diversity is to portray the richness in approaches that exists and to design a process of wisdom formation in human sexuality that cuts across divergent theological perspectives.

There is an orthodox theological approach to human sexuality. In this approach, the theological doctrines and creeds of a particular faith tradition are the starting point. Orthodox approaches are considered traditional and are characterized by a heterosexual view of marital sex for the purposes of procreation as normative.[8] Sexual pleasuring in marriage may not be emphasized, and practices such as masturbation, artificial birth control, abortion, homosexuality, bisexuality, oral or anal sex, and premarital sexual relationships are considered to be immoral. The statements about human sexuality reflect the consensus of a particular faith body that is based on its established doctrines.

Another approach to the theology of sexuality comes from those persons who rely on developments during the Enlightenment and post-Enlightenment period. Here the starting point is not tradition or Scripture. Rather, the starting point is human experience and reason. Thus, the experience of people in sexual matters becomes the source of wisdom. Such approaches are usually relationally based where relationships with others are highly valued.[9] This approach emphasizes that moral laws were made to guide and inform human relationships. Thus, sexual intercourse is not just for procreation, nor is there anything inherently evil about any sexual act as long as the motives and consequences of sexual acts conform to certain ethical and relational principles. This view highly values human experience and right decision making. Justice, equality, reciprocity, mutuality, and the dignity of each person are highly respected in this orientation.

Related to the approaches that begin with human experience are the liberation, feminist, and womanist approaches to human sexuality. As with the Enlightenment approach, human experience is the starting point. Liberation, feminist, and womanist orientations differ from the Enlightenment approaches, however, in the fact that the European male experience is not normative. Rather, particular racial, ethnic, and gender experiences become a source of wisdom. In addition, the ways in which sex and oppression interact within the racial, ethnic, and gender experiences of oppression are also important sources of wisdom. Moreover, the heterosexual domination and the oppressiveness that it fosters are also part of the wisdom that comes from these approaches.

Process approaches to wisdom about sexuality begins with human experience. Process approaches, however, like those that begin with human experience, move from human experience to theology in formulating its wisdom. They begin with the organismic dimension of human experience grounded in human evolution and then move to theologies that focus on the creation of God. The creation story in Genesis 1 is privileged more than the creation story found in Genesis 2 and 3.

There is a neo-orthodox approach to sexuality that is called critical realism. This approach privileges the understanding of human sexuality that derives from the second creation story in the book of Genesis. This story is about the corruption of creation by the Fall, and how sexuality was consequently distorted. Thus, sexuality is viewed as a fallen dimension that needs redemption by God.

The final approach to human sexuality is the narrative theological one. It emphasizes the essential participation of each person in the faith community and in its stories. The community's faith stories are privileged with regard to sexuality, and particularly the stories of grace and inclusion are given primary focus. In this approach, the unfolding stories of salvation and inclusion of all persons in God's family and grace are emphasized. Thus each person is called to shape his or her understanding of sexuality based on the unfolding story of God's salvation.

This last approach seems to cut across all the divergent

approaches. Rather than focus on doctrinal propositions and essential normative statements, the emphasis is on how participation in story shapes character and attitudes. Therefore the emphasis is on process and on becoming. One is formed in wisdom about sexuality as one participates. Normative and propositional statements are still involved, but they become part of the narrative process where grace becomes privileged. In the section regarding passing on wisdom regarding sexuality, the emphasis will be on narrative approaches as inclusive of other approaches.

Science, Sexuality, Sexual Practices, and Wisdom

From ancient times, philosophers have held that it is possible to increase our wisdom and, ultimately, control human sexual expression by following the tenets of science. The watchwords of the scientific method are *validity* (measuring the greatest dimension of truth possible) and *reliability* (measuring the greatest degree of consistency possible). Scientific tests are supposed to measure whatever the chosen behavior both accurately and consistently occurs every time a test is used.

If one would ask whether the scientific method has been applied to the study of human sexuality, the answer would be not until recently. We know that human sexuality is similar to other physiological drives (the need for air, water, sleep, food, shelter from extreme climates, and so forth). And we know that thwarting these basic drives can lead to irreparable psycho-physical harm and eventually death. Yet our sexuality is qualitatively different. This part of our biology is melded into and out of one's culture. Indeed, every human being reflects his or her contextually defined socialization process. An inherent part of the socialization process in black communities has been historically to regard sexual matters as a taboo subject. Sexual matters have typically been construed as a private concern that is supported by the view even of Christians that, although one is accountable to God for how one acts on sexual matters, the actions are still a private affair. As a result, if the matter of sex or sexuality is raised in or beyond church bounds, the learned response is, "We'd best leave that subject alone. It is a matter between the person and God."

Because of disproportionate incidence of sexually transmitted diseases (STDs) and HIV/AIDS in the black community, the silence is being broken. Scientists are giving much attention to tracing the causes of the disease, to risk-reduction research, and to methods of reducing the incidence in community settings. Indeed, the work of the scientific community is immensely important not simply to breaking the "code of silence," but to black churches' promotion of black people's wisdom formation. Attention to wisdom formation requires these churches' promotion of people's conscious awareness of truths about the disease and their commitments to responsible preventive practices.

Loretta Sweet Jemmott and her associates summarize data showing that black Americans compose 37 percent of the 733,000-plus AIDS cases reported through 1999 in the United States, with black women representing one of the fastest growing subgroups of new HIV/AIDS cases.[10] Moreover, 15 percent of all HIV infections among black males, and 24 percent of these infections among black females, occurred in those from age 13 to 24.[11] In addition, studies show that "although there are nonsexual means of contracting HIV, including injection drug use (IDU) and blood transfusions, the worldwide AIDS pandemic has been largely fueled by sexual transmission. Among African Americans in the United States, sexual transmission is one of the most common routes of HIV transmission, particularly among women and adolescents."[12]

Health authorities also indicate that gonorrhea and chlamydia are two sexually transmitted diseases (STDs), or diseases contracted by sexual contact, that disproportionately affect African Americans. Cohall and Bannister emphasize that both of these diseases can be treated with antibiotics. However, long-term serious consequences such as pelvic inflammatory disease, ectopic pregnancy and sterility for women, and orchitis and sterility for men can result when treatment is delayed or not sought.[13] Again, wisdom formation requires breaking the silence about these types of STDs as well as other forms such as genital herpes or herpes simplex type II, and Hepatitis C, which are incurable. Wisdom formation entails giving frank attention to the need for widespread screening for these diseases especially among the young, and of engaging youth and their families in equally straightforward discussions about the risks of casual or recreational sex and the sureness of abstinence. Yet it is certainly true that straightforward discussion alone will not make the difference.

Clearly, in light of the documented high incidence of STDs and HIV/AIDS, particularly among the young in the black community, there is need for an emphasis on wisdom formation that focuses on effectively reducing risk-related sexual behavior. In this regard, some behavioral scientists propose a theory of planned behavior to bring about effective HIV risk-reducing sexual practices. This theory underscores the role of behavioral intentions, normative beliefs, and control beliefs as strong determinants of risk-reducing sexual practices.[14] Behavioral intentions refer to an individual's conscious decision to employ risk-reducing behaviors. But forming and acting on these intentions depend on the individual's normative beliefs, including whether she/he evaluates the behavior positively, whether she/he believes significant others would approve of the behavior, and whether she/he believes the behavior will have favorable consequences. Control beliefs refer to the extent of the individual's conviction in her/his ability to actually carry out a specific behavior.[15]

Engaging Wisdom-directed Conversation Through Uses of Contemporary Novels

A promising way of stimulating conversation on matters pertaining to sexuality and sex is through the use of contemporary novels. The importance of this method of drawing people's attention to and involvement in these matters lies in its phenomenological impact or what we make of the insights disclosed in novels. Novels are creative means of bringing to consciousness experiences related to sexuality and sexual practice, values and norms undergirding the experiences, as well as meanings of these experiences for current-day values formation and sexual practice. Particularly in regards to sexuality, novels disclose and can place us in touch with the subjective experience of sexual desire. The key issue concerns what the person experiences as desire and how he or she attempts to understand or bring meaning to desire.

Desire here is understood as the confluence of the sexual urge with the object that exists to satisfy this urge. Sexual desire is a physiological drive built into human existence, and how it gets expressed is developmentally shaped by the everyday experiences and interaction with others. Sexual desire also relates to passion for or desire for a partner sexually, which includes sex as well as relational intimacy.[16] The key issue is that it is not possible to isolate sexual desire, physiologically, from relationship issues. Physiology and human interaction combine to form a complex whole.

The key philosophical issue in the phenomenology of sexuality is how a person validates his or her own sexual desire when this desire and its expression are clearly different from the established social norm. Theologically, the issue relating to sexual desire is the validation of sexual desire and its expression when they differ from established theological and ethical norms. Another concern is how much weight should we give to traditional notions of desire and our own experiences of sexual desire.

Additional concerns relate to how we affirm ourselves as human beings when our sexual desires and their expression deviate from the norm. Contemporary phenomenology of sexuality describes the inner subjective processes of human beings as they attempt to bring meaning and understanding to sexual desire.

The Novels of E. Lynn Harris

E. Lynn Harris has written a half dozen novels exploring the inner subjective experiences of men who engage in homosexual and bisexual activity.[17] The novels appear to present the authentic struggles that homosexuals and bisexuals have with establishing sexual identities based on sexual desire and the need for genuine relationships with others. Sexual desire and the preference for a sexual partner of the same sex or the opposite sex are presented as complex and even tragic at times. Yet what emerges from the six novels is the fact that at least some homosexuals find fulfillment in a couple relationship where there is sexual intercourse as well as genuine love, respect, commitment, and fidelity. The novels do not glamorize homosexual relationships at the expense of exploring the real emotional difficulties homosexual and bisexual persons confront. The novels present excellent examples and commentaries on family of origin issues and problems that homosexual and bisexual men face with their families, friends, and relatives.

The experiences related to sexual orientation, sexual desire, and sexual intercourse from same-sex partners can be a source of wisdom. Some feel that the experiences people have should override all other considerations in the formation of wisdom. Harris' novels convey that wisdom formation from the standpoint of homosexuality and bisexuality is an extremely private reality that no one but the subject can reason through even when the wisdom learned is not consistent with established community norms and conventions.

The Work of Pearl Cleage

Wisdom that comes from experience also can confirm conventional wisdom that exists in tradition and Scripture. One of Pearl Cleage's works focuses on how the experiences of a woman with the HIV virus led to the development of a relationship of true love and sexual intercourse within the ideal of marriage. Cleage's novel *What Looks Like Crazy on an Ordinary Day* is about how ongoing experiences in life teach wisdom.[18] It focuses on the meaning of true love and whether one should wait until one finds true love before engaging in sexual intercourse. Ava is the chief protagonist who is diagnosed with the HIV virus she contracted from a man whom she did not like or love. She is running away from intimacy, but when she contracts the HIV virus, she has to decide how she is going to live the rest of her life. She returns to her hometown, where she reconnects with her family and finds true love despite having the HIV virus. The book is a positive commentary on what is possible in life despite a potential death sentence.

The novel emphasizes wisdom on several levels. The real question is whether it is possible to be celibate or to refuse to settle for just sex until one's true love comes along. The reality portrayed is that this is very difficult and almost impossible for most human beings except for the very lucky. The wisdom that is portrayed in the novel is that true love is possible even when one settles for just sex. At the same time, however, the book also affirms the wisdom that settling for less should be avoided because of the relational difficulty, disenchantment, and self-abrogation that can result.

Narrative as Key in Wisdom-directed Conversation

Uses of a narrative orientation to sexual and spiritual wisdom can assist people to take seriously all sources of human wisdom, namely theology, philosophy, ethics, and science. The narrative orientation emphasizes that wisdom is formed through full participation in the life of a particular community. Full participation means interacting with significant others, hearing and telling personal and communal stories, and enacting particular rituals that shape the character of individuals and those in the community.

A narrative orientation focuses on the full participation of all persons regardless of sexual orientation in the unfolding drama of salvation. The key emphasis is not on the use of propositional rules, but on how communal participation in the faith community and its story shapes the moral character of the person. Such character formation takes seriously the relational dimensions of character formation; and, although there is recognition of the privacy and primacy of one's relationship with God in sexual matters, the goal of wisdom formation is to invite persons to grapple with the very lives they live. It means inviting persons into a quest for the meaning of being a community of Christian character and for what it means to act, individually, as Christians in every area of our lives. This is crucial particularly with regard to decisions individuals and couples make with regard to sexual orientation and premarital sex. Issues regarding adultery and multiple sex partners may also be regarded as private, but the private boundaries are difficult to maintain due to the fact that more than two people are involved.

In the narrative approach, individuals are viewed as agents who do select, for good or ill, from a variety of sources in deciding how they will address issues of sex and sexuality. Individuals are agents in their own formation of wisdom. Thus, it is important that individuals are participants in a faith community where they are invited to consider their formation of sexual wisdom. It is essential, as well, to recognize that sexual wisdom formation is a lifelong process that responds to the life transitions and crises that people experience.

During a lifetime of the formation of sexual wisdom, a person can privilege a variety of sources of wisdom formation. For example, the starting point for wisdom formation could be theology, philosophy, ethics, or science. However, none of these starting points can proceed without serious consideration of the actual story one lives, where this story is headed, why, and what to do about it if another direction is warranted.

Black Churches as Wisdom Guides

The alarming incidence of HIV/AIDS in the black community, and especially among black youth and young adults, demands a response from the faith community. Black churches across the denominational spectrum and local congregations must become intensely committed to developing and implementing ongoing prevention-focused educational strategies to reverse the current trend. The "Fact Sheet: Faith Communities and HIV/AIDS," shows that faith-based initiatives tend to focus on primary care or support services, but offer prevention and education programs to a lesser degree.[19] Yet education exists as a critical guide to persons' acting wisely in the face of this devastating disease. How may black churches become wisdom guides?

Churches take on the role as wisdom guides through their access of resources for educational ministries focused on HIV prevention. Several types of materials are available from national faith-based organizations, among which are the following:

- A curriculum entitled "Affirming a Future with Hope: HIV and Substance Abuse Prevention for African American Communities of Faith," produced by the Interdenominational Theological Center Health Education Leadership Project (H.E.L.P.), Atlanta, Georgia.
- A curriculum entitled "Affirming Ourselves, Saving Lives: AIDS Awareness and Prevention Education," graded for all age levels from preschool through senior adults, produced by United Church Press, The United Church of Christ, Cleveland, Ohio.
- A list of resources entitled "The Congregation: A Community of Care and Healing, HIV/AIDS Awareness Resources," produced by the Presbyterian Church (USA).
- The Balm in Gilead, based in New York City, represents the

seven historic black denominations and provides leadership designed to assist black churches' response to HIV/AIDS.

Besides HIV prevention education, much attention is being turned to the role of churches as wisdom guides in sex education. For example, there is evidence that the level of awareness of this need is rising in the wider faith community. According to Louie Palmer, "Faith-based sex education is taking off across the nation, [guided by] the principle that sexuality is God-given, an integral part of being human. . . . Rather than offering a litany of do's and don'ts, religious leaders are increasingly interested in helping adolescents see their physicality in spiritual terms."[20] Where it has not already happened, black churches are called to join this effort.

The importance of the churches' wisdom-forming role in providing sex education lies in the fact that public schools often do not offer it, and it is all too often a taboo subject in the home. Although faith-based sex educators view the home as the primary context for guiding young people in matters of sexuality and sexual practice, they contend that the faith community should support parents in this task.[21] Whatever the context, according to a United Nations report, comprehensive HIV/AIDS and sex education programs resulted in program participants' delay in beginning sexual activity, reducing the number of partners, or decreasing their rate of STDs and unplanned pregnancy.[22] Helpful resources that represent a broad perspective include the following:

- "Male and Female: Blessed by God," a curriculum for grades 10-12 in biblical theological approaches to sexuality, relationships, dating, sexually explicit materials, sexual abuse, and STDs, is produced by The United Methodist Church and available through Cokesbury Bookstore, Nashville, Tennessee. A similar resource for adolescents grades 7-9, entitled "Our Sexuality: God's Gift," edited by Brannon L. Thurston, is also available from Cokesbury.
- The guide "Family Sexuality Education: A Course for Parents," which includes activities for parents with children and early adolescents, written by the Rev. Joe Leonard, is available from Judson Press, Valley Forge, Pennsylvania.
- An annotated bibliography focused on a comprehensive

approach to sex education can be obtained from The Sexuality Information and Education Council of the United States (SIECUS), in New York City.

In conclusion, three concerns shaped this chapter. The first identified the need for the church in general to be a wisdom guide in the areas of sexuality and sexual activity. The second involved the sources of such wisdom. The third involved the role of educational ministry as a wisdom guide in matters of sexuality. This chapter affirmed that the black church provides a rich language for conversations taking place about sexuality; yet there is the need for the ofttimes noticeable silence on sexual matters to be broken for the sake of our engagement in straight talk about sex and sexuality. The narrative approach is a compelling one that invites people from youth to adults to look closely at their own stories and the moral character that ushers from the faith community in which they participate. It can be said that we live in a culture today where people need help in bringing perspective to their sexual lives, given the prominent attention given to sex in our culture. There are many languages that inform the conversations that take place within all of us with regard to sexuality. The role of the church in providing a safe setting to help us bring a wise perspective to our lives will continue to be essential.

CHAPTER 9

Forming a Spirituality
of Wisdom

Jonathan Jackson, Jr.

*Spirituality is a state of being grounded in the Spirit of God and God's love
expressed in Jesus the Christ. . . . Spirit needs a home with large spaces in order
to be free to move, to grow, and to expand in our lives.*
—Michael Dash, Jonathan Jackson, and Stephen Rasor[1]

In the seeming inevitable and troublesome desert places of our
lives, we thirst for wisdom. But our thirst is also for a spirituality
that undergirds our wisdom. We thirst for wisdom that is undergirded by a spirituality that makes possible our creation of a place
of joy and celebration even in our personal struggles and in a
world torn apart with great human suffering.[2] Quenching this
thirst happens through the formation of a spirituality of wisdom
that centers on our ongoing creation of a space for God, the ground
of our being. It is our discovery and rediscovery that "in [God's]
hand is the life of every living thing and the breath of every human
being" (Job 12:10). It is our discerning where and how God is leading us toward a more fully developed participation with God in
the world.

The spirituality of wisdom leads us to Jesus Christ, the one
whom God sent to give us a "drink of the one Spirit" that will satisfy us, or a drink of living water, water of hope. It leads us toward
living a story after the pattern of Jesus Christ and in accordance

with the gifts given to us by the Spirit of God for the common good (1 Corinthians 12:7). We discover our interconnected and interrelated life in community and our responsibility to one another even with our varieties of gifts and services: "If one member suffers, all suffer together with it; if one member is honored, all rejoice together with it" (1 Corinthians 12:26). This spirituality of wisdom leads us not simply to an ongoing supply of waters of hope. It makes possible our very experience of blossoms in the desert. In this chapter, we will explore in more detail what a spirituality of wisdom is, how we form it and sustain it, and how a spirituality of wisdom gets expressed in our everyday living. Moreover, some attention will be given to the role of the church's educational ministry in promoting the formation of a spirituality of wisdom.

Exploring a Spirituality of Wisdom

Wisdom formation is about our forming a spirituality of wisdom; and wisdom is the praxis or our action and reflection on our spirituality of wisdom. Christians' seeking wisdom is accompanied by our seeking and reflecting on a spirituality of wisdom that is different from technical or scientific knowledge. Scientific knowledge deals with finitude or that which is limited to what can be seen and verified. But a spirituality of wisdom deals with the infiniteness of God and God's creation, which encompasses all that is, all that lies beyond what is observable and verifiable, yet brings everything together. A spirituality of wisdom is wholeness-centered. This spirituality enables us to see the whole picture—to look at all of life and to put life in perspective. It empowers us to see the wholeness of life and to drink of the fountain of life and hope in the midst of struggle. Thus wisdom and spirituality cannot be separated. The two are inextricably tied together, and they are bound together in such a way that spirituality can be said to be the place where wisdom sits.

A spirituality of wisdom centers on our knowing the source of wisdom that goes beyond the brain and the totality of the person to the Creator of persons and all that is. At the same time, a spirituality of wisdom relies on our awareness of the human community as a source of wisdom and counsel. Wisdom comes from our relationships with one another in the human community. Wisdom forms in and is advised by our family relationships. It forms in and is enlightened by our participation in the faith community and the community at large. Our spirituality of wisdom derives from an all-embracing vision of the Divine-human encounter and the encounter of humans with humans. The latter notion of the encounter of humans with humans is a particularly important added dimension to the Divine-human encounter in black spirituality because of the primacy of the group and the communal character that comes of the traditional African worldview.[3] But what we often glean from the wisdom found in the black community is, in fact, a spirituality of wisdom that is revealed in people's stories of their own Divine-human encounter. Let me illustrate.

I grew up around deeply spiritual people and I learned a great deal from them. In their lives, I saw the epitome of a deep spirituality and powerful wisdom that could not be separated and that revealed the closeness of their relationship with God and Jesus Christ in the deserts of their lives. One of these people was my great-aunt who was the aunt of my mother, who is still alive at age ninety-one. My great-aunt would say to me, "Son, my mother was a slave, and my mother's aunt was a slave. She was beaten by the master. She was beaten so, that she just prayed, and prayed, and prayed. She knew that she could pray. She prayed so hard that it reached a point in her life where she didn't have to pray anymore. All she had to do was say 'Jesus.' "

My great-aunt's story demonstrates that wisdom comes through suffering, which sensitizes a person and makes him or her open and aware of the spiritual presence that abides at the deeper level of Christian reality. The story also invites us to consider that pain, suffering, and hurt can propel us out of ourselves toward wisdom rather than pull us into a self-negating posture.

My own spirituality of wisdom received counsel from the spirituality of wisdom of my great-aunt. I heard my great-aunt's reference to the One who had quenched her mother's thirst and that now relieved her own dryness in life's wilderness. I heard that their calling on that One gave strength to continue on. Hearing my great-aunt's story alerted me that her mother was in a dialogue with God through Jesus Christ; and my awareness of the dialogue that continued in my aunt's life as well as its regenerating effect informed my own formation of a spirituality of wisdom.

Spirituality of Wisdom as an Awakening

The formation of a spirituality of wisdom may be likened to our awakening from sleep. This awakening is not so much from a physical sleep. Rather, it is from our diminished state of awareness. Anthony de Mello, a Jesuit priest, refers to the sleep state as the nature of human existence that summons not simply the "wake-up call" but the very reason for waking up. A story that illustrates this matter of waking up is about an individual who was sleeping one morning and the father said, "Son, wake up, it's time to go to school." But the son said, "Daddy, I don't want to go to school today." The father replied, "You've got to get up and go to school. Come on, son, wake up." The father proceeded to pull the cover off the son, but the son pulled the cover back and said, "No, Father, I do not want to go to school because the children don't like me. The teachers don't like me, either. School is boring and I am not going to school today." The father stood and looked down on his son and said, "Well, son, I can think of some reasons why you ought to go to school. First of all, you should go to school because you simply ought to go. Second, you're forty-five years old, and you're not done with school yet. But third, my son, you are the principal."[4]

The story symbolizes how the matter of waking up is of extreme importance in our lives. The formation of our spirituality of wisdom is our waking up to the challenges and calls to us all to extend our love and service to others. And, importantly, this kind of waking up that forms our spirituality of wisdom emanates from our awakening to the Spirit of God and our opening our whole selves—body, mind, and spirit—to God.[5]

Awakening to Awareness of God. The formation of a spirituality of wisdom that derives from our rousing from sleep centers on our coming to awareness of the all-wise and ever-present God. We come to recognize God as Creator, Redeemer, and Sustainer of our faith. We become conscious of God's creation of our individual selves, others, our environment, and all of creation. God becomes known to us as the ground of our being, the author of life and community, and source of existence as we know it. We acknowledge the parenthood of God and the kinship of all peoples.[6] Moreover, as Michael Dash, Steven Rasor, and I indicate in our book, *Hidden Wholeness*: "We discover the glory of God in the life and ministry of Jesus. We rediscover God's creative purpose for humankind in this man, Jesus . . . [and that] the way he related to others models for us [the] intended relationship God desires."[7]

In our wakefulness, we also come to know that God does not leave us alone. God remains present in our private and communal lives as friend, advocate, and Divine presence. This knowing gives us the strength we need "in community and in individual acts of courage, through the perpetual remembrance of the truth of Christ—through the power of the Holy Spirit."[8]

I like to look at our wakefulness as our recognition of the teaching God and of our seeking and discerning the wisdom God gives us to traverse life's daily sojourn, including the desert places. The prayer of the psalmist that acknowledges this quality of God and our need for it throughout our lives comes to mind: "So teach us to number our days that we may apply our hearts to wisdom" (Psalm 90:12).[9]

Awakening to the Importance of a Spiritual Foundation. A spirituality of wisdom that ensues from our waking up becomes an anchored spirituality or a spirituality that has a very deep foundation in God through Jesus Christ and the Holy Spirit and the gospel that is disclosed in Scripture. It is well known that a central aspect of black spirituality is its strong emphasis on the Bible. The sermonic event in black worship engages us in the dramatic retelling of a biblical story or moving declaration of a text. Whether in worship, Bible study, church school, or private devotions, the point of the focus on Scripture is our wakefulness not simply to the foundation provided by the Word and the message of the past articulated by the Word, but to what it indicates for the present and life's potential.[10] The point is also that we care for this foundation through intentional response to it through action in life and through the spiritual disciplines such as prayer and contemplation.

One incident in my own life brought forth my keen awareness of the importance of a deep foundation and care given to my formation of a spirituality of wisdom. I will never forget when our house burned. It didn't burn completely to ashes, but a portion of it burned and the other part was heavily damaged by smoke. Our house had to be rebuilt, beginning from the structural or foundation level. I remember going to check on the progress of the workers. They had done the work on the foundation and the frame of the house. Experts were also present who were spraying pesticide around and on the foundation to assure protection against termites. I asked one of the technicians, "Why are you using the pesticide at the foundation level when you are going to cover the house with concrete, wood, and other materials?" He answered, "If we do this now and at the foundation level, it will alleviate termites and other bugs from invading your house. If we do not do it now, the house could be infested and destroyed after it is finished."

In short, the significance of this story in my life is its illustration of the critical need to care for the foundation of our spirituality of wisdom.

Awakening to the Nature of Our Life's Direction. It is said, if you know where you are going, generally you can get there. But discerning the direction for our lives is not always easy. There is often a challenge associated with being awake to where God is leading us. History is replete with examples of individuals or groups who considered themselves to be aware of God's intentions for their lives, but which called into grave question what they discerned from God. The tragic attack on the World Trade Center in New York City is an example that will be forever carved in the soul of a nation and the world.

I, along with Michael Dash and Stephen Rasor, have said in *Hidden Wholeness* that, for Christians, "perceiving God's will and having the courage to be obedient to it are also challenges. The 'courage to be' (Tillich) in the world as a follower of Christ Jesus, in a . . . daring fashion, is called for in our society—yet often unheeded."[11] Our formation of a spirituality of wisdom that encompasses our waking up to God's intentions for our lives requires us to aspire to discern God's activity. Moreover, it compels us to dare to be courageous as individuals and whole communities in facing difficult, thorny, and even life-threatening issues in the desert place such as economic, racial or other injustice, sexism, classism, ageism, world hunger, and war. Wakefulness means that we *will* dare to be courageous. We *will* choose to be obedient.[12]

But, again, it is terribly important to be mindful that our daring and our choosing must be guided by the model of Jesus Christ. The formation of our spirituality of wisdom rests on this awareness.

Let me share another story. There was a little boy who was bothering his father, who was a pastor. The father was in the process of finishing his sermon for Sunday worship. So he gave his son a piece of paper with a picture of the world on it, tore it, and made it into a puzzle. He told the son, "Son, put this together." The father knew that this task would keep the son busy for a long time. However, to the father's surprise, the son returned within a few minutes and said, "Is this what you wanted me to do, Daddy?" The father said, "How did you put the puzzle together so quickly?" The little boy replied, "On the other side of this picture of the world was a picture of Jesus. So, look what I did, Daddy. I put the picture of Jesus together." Yet the model of Jesus Christ must not be what Thomas Merton calls "our own image, a projection of our own aspirations, desires, and ideals."[13] We cannot imitate the Jesus Christ we have in our own imaginations; and it is likewise difficult for us to grasp fully what it means to live like him by our efforts. As Merton suggests, our dependence on our own ideas, judgment, and efforts to reproduce the life of Christ will result in our being "so stiff and artificial and so dead."[14] Yes, we must read and study the Gospels, but it is more than comprehending what appears in them that will make the difference in our courageously living after the model of Jesus Christ. Following his model depends on our knowing and expecting the Spirit of God will teach us who he is, will form Christ in us, and will transform us into Christ's likeness.[15]

The formation of our spirituality of wisdom surely means that we become wakeful that God's intention for our lives is revealed in the direction Jesus Christ provides. When we put together the image of Jesus Christ in our hearts, minds and spirits, we receive a direction for life. We want to keep before us this image.

An Awakening to Time in the Formation of Spirituality of Wisdom. Time is pivotal in our formation of a spirituality of wisdom. In fact, we human beings are defined by our temporality. We often think of time in terms of *chronos*, which is time measured according to calendar and clock time. Our awareness of this view of time raises our consciousness of the movement of our lives across the developmental stages. The formation of a spirituality of wisdom is not the province of a single stage. It is the worthy task of every stage beginning with childhood and proceeding through old age.

We will recall that chapter 2 gives us guidance regarding the significance of stories, proverbs, parables, and songs as means of heightening awareness of cultural views of the faith and formation of a spirituality of wisdom. Moreover, based on what we have already read in chapter 3, the children's and youth's awakening to wisdom with a firm spiritual basis must happen in cross-generational communication or through the help of wise adults. Moreover, according to chapters 5 and 6, as males and females mature, their own spiritual growth that becomes expressed in wise decisions and actions in life depend on their continuing consciousness of God's direction for their lives. Chapter 7 reminds us that, as we move in and through middle and older adulthood, the awakening we need is for new life meaning and our place in it. And chapter 8 emphasizes that awakening to a wise perspective on sex and sexuality requires straight talk by all at every age/stage.

Yet, even as we consider the idea of *chronos* as it relates to the formation of a spirituality of wisdom, we must also recognize that we are not fixed beings. It is not simply the formation of a spirituality of wisdom in a given age/stage that is the issue here. Wisdom that develops from a spiritual foundation is cumulative so that how, really, it has developed and how we have actually lived our lives as the result of it is completely describable only at our death. Of course all along life's way there must be abundant reflection on what has and is happening in our lives as well as what potentials there are for living the faith forward. But there is a unique retrospective dimension toward life's completion that awakens us to the threads of continuity, change, purpose, meaning, triumphs, failures in our lives, and ultimately to our arrival at ego-integrity rather than despair.

Chronos is not the only view of time that guides our view of what "waking up" means in our formation of a spirituality of wisdom. *Kairos* is an understanding of time that refers to significant points in our lives in which we awake to the call of God and respond to God. However, our awakening as Christians is not to an awareness of one view of time over another, because, for us, all time finds its focus and fulfillment in Christ. This awareness leads to a related consciousness, to use Lawrence O. Richard's words, "that we use our moments of time wisely, sensing the eternal significance that our relationship with Jesus brings to all time."[16]

The Storied Journey of Forming a Spirituality of Wisdom

We live our lives as a story that unfolds scene by scene from before our birth until our death. Our life stories neither unfold in an altogether predictable nor completely smooth way. In these stories, there are twists and turns, trials and tribulations, challenges and triumphs. As black people, the story has been characterized by the "howlin' wilderness" or desert experience that, over the years, created our soul's search for peace with justice and a yearning for a sense of "home" in a weary land. Historically, the formation of a spirituality of wisdom was the way into that "home" in the wilderness where there was spiritual food for the hungry soul and refreshing water from the fountain that shall never run dry. In the midst of suffering, the "wildaness" became "filled with trees, springs, lakes, and fruit. The metaphorical wilderness was filled with music, dance, and preaching and was thus transformed into a garden."[17] Moreover, the garden was inhabited by a communal people who sang communal songs that affirmed a communal identity and a communal wisdom, as Yolanda Smith suggests in chapter 2.

Black people's experience of the blossoming of the desert into a garden, transformed by God's hands, and by black people's wise engagement in their own liberation struggle, has been the dominating theme of black people's spirituality of wisdom. However, the fact is that too many people experience the ravages of continuing and new "deserts," the most pernicious of which is the nihilistic threat or the loss of hope and the absence of meaning.[18] This reality in the unfolding story of black people demands attention to the question, *How do we assure and sustain the presence of a spirituality of wisdom in the third millennium?*

I want to suggest that there must first be some clarity regarding the difference between spirituality and Christian spirituality. A life story that centers on Christian spirituality is communal. This communal dimension is sorely needed in the present busy, individualistic, competitive society in which we live, where families cease to eat together, neighbors don't know one another, and the struggle for economic sufficiency and gain prevails. We need desperately to recognize and affirm the interconnectedness of our families and communities, local and global and to recognize the necessity of our reaching out toward one another. Wisdom demands our creating environments where hospitality, healing, and wholeness happen. Yet, in a real sense, we cannot create these environments by ourselves. Yes, wisdom must compel us to take responsibility for living out our stories in word and deed in response to God's call to repair God's community and God's creation. But to the extent that we are spiritually anchored in God, we remember that it is God with us who gives us eyes to see and a compass to follow the direction toward communal wholeness.[19]

Second, I want to propose that a spirituality of wisdom must be formed and practiced individually. I do not want this to be construed as a contradiction to the communal dimension just presented. Rather, what I want to emphasize here is that unless we have a clear sense of our own identity in God as well our recognition of and commitment to respond to the teaching God, the communal wholeness toward which we must direct our lives in the third millennium will surely be thwarted. The revision of the human story from brokenness to wholeness—whether in family, church, local community, or world—must begin with each one of us.

Finally, I want to point out that the formation and sustenance of a spirituality of wisdom must be undergirded by the black churches' educational ministry efforts. The task of educational ministry in the black church is to assure the formation of wisdom and the spiritual foundations for it. The emphasis is a holistic orientation to wisdom formation that seeks to bring attention to the impact of wisdom formation for carrying out every ministry of the church, including the church's ministry of teaching, preaching, worship, witnessing, and service.

In carrying out these efforts, the churches' emphasis must not be centered on simply getting over knowledge to black people. The formation and sustenance of holistic wisdom formation requires more than dispensing an aggregate set of facts, which may be likened to "dumping gravel" on people's heads. Rather, the role of the churches is to evoke in black people a seriousness about the church's ministries and about the self's servant leadership in them. The servant leadership toward which the educational ministry must be directed is modeled demonstrably by Jesus' presence with people and worship with his followers, care for hurting persons, regard for the downtrodden and the needy, and his taking on the role of servant even to the point of washing his disciples' feet. The formation of a spirituality of wisdom that leads to black people's servant leadership after the model of Jesus also requires an emphasis on the church's ministry within and beyond its walls. The preparation of servant leaders through the churches' educational ministry must be for the care, uplift, and transformation of people within the congregation and in the public sphere. The preparation is for servant leadership in a church without walls. At the same time, the formation of a spirituality of wisdom through the black churches' educational ministry must guide black people not simply toward love of and service to others but toward love and care of self.

Mention has been made in earlier chapters about the importance of storytelling and story-listening as educational ministry approaches that contribute to the formation of wisdom of black people. The reality is that a story is a teacher. What I want to add here is simply that Jesus provides the model. Jesus was an educator about people, the world, and God. How did Jesus teach? Jesus taught through the narrative means such as the parable, the metaphor, and the story. In so doing, he was able to "unhinge" religion so that it would reveal what God is like. The use of narrative means, then, is of extreme importance in helping people form a spirituality of wisdom; and in using the narrative orientation, the essential question to be asked by educational ministry leaders is, *How does the story affect my story and your story?* When we are able to mesh our stories with the cosmic story of God, then we begin in earnest to shape a spirituality of wisdom.

The Self as Starting Point in Forming a Spirituality of Wisdom: An Invitation

The formation of a spirituality of wisdom is like drinking from a stream of water in the desert that never dries up. To stay alive, you must continue to drink the water.[20] In this closing section, I invite you to approach the water through several experiences of self-awareness. I am inviting you to do so because I firmly believe that the formation of a spirituality of wisdom begins with each one of us. We cannot guide anyone beyond where we are ourselves. These activities may be done in a group setting with a leader who guides the group through each step.[21]

Moving Toward Self-awareness

- Find a quiet space. Turn off the radio and television.
- Let go of all tension and uptightness. Think relaxation in your legs and arms.
- Allow yourself to feel at home in your seat.
- Close your eyes as a means of eliminating all visual images.
- Slow down your breathing and form peaceful thoughts.
- Move to the following meditation.

Meditation on Drinking from the Stream of Water in the Desert

- Bring to mind some blockages that have prevented you from experiencing a sense of wholeness. You may want to write these blocks down in a journal.
- Envision Jesus coming toward you and then sitting beside you.
- Ask Jesus what you want and need to remove the blockages.
- In your mind's eye, see Jesus touching your shoulder and saying, " 'Lo, I am with you always, even unto the ends of the earth.' I will be with you and acting in your life for the removal of your blocks to wholeness."

Meditation on Knowing the Presence of God

- Find a quiet place. Turn off the radio and television.
- Let go of all tension and uptightness. Think relaxation in your legs and arms.
- Allow yourself to feel at home in your seat.
- Close your eyes in order to eliminate all visual images.
- Listen for noise in and outside the room and simply "be" in the presence of those sounds. Imagine yourself as "going with the beat."

- Recite the following:
  "Be still and know that I am God."
  "Be still and know that I am"
  "Be still and know that I"
  "Be still and know that"
  "Be still and know"
  "Be still"
  "Be"
  "Be"
  "Be"

Notes

Preface

1. Jerry Ortiz y Pino, "Whatever Happened to Wisdom?" originally appeared in the *Santa Fe Reporter* and reprinted in "The Wisdom Page," http://www.cop.com/info/wisdompg.html#10.

Introduction

1. Some of the publications focused on wisdom in black perspective are the following: Robert Fleming, *The Wisdom of the Elders: Inspiring Reflections from the Heart of African American Culture* (New York: Ballantine Books, 1996); Diane J. Johnson, ed., *The Proud Sisters: The Wisdom and Wit of African American Women* (Peter Pauper Press, 1995); Venice Johnson, ed., *Heart Full of Grace: A Thousand Years of Black Wisdom* (New York: Fireside, 1997); Julia Stewart, *African Proverbs and Wisdom* (Secaucus, N.J.: Citadel Press, Carol Publishing Group, 1998); Cheryl Willis Hudson and Wade Hudson, *Kids' Book of Wisdom: Quotes from the African American Tradition* (East Orange, N.J.: Just Us Books, 1997); Jay David, ed., *Songs of Wisdom: Quotations from Famous African Americans of the Twentieth Century* (New York: William Morrow, 1998); and Eugene Seals and Matthew Parker, eds., *Called to Lead: Wisdom for the Next Generation of African American Leaders* (Chicago: Moody Press, 1995).

2. The quote appears in the publisher's commentary on the back cover of Robert Fleming's *The Wisdom of the Elders: Inspiring Reflections from the Heart of African American Culture* (New York: Ballantine Books, 1996).

3. Charles M. Johnston, "The Wisdom of Limits," *In Context* (a Quarterly of Humane Sustainable Culture), http://context.org/ICLIB/IC32/Johnston.htm, 1.

4. See Cornel West, *Race Matters* (New York: Vintage Books, 1994), 15-31; C. Eric Lincoln and Lawrence Mamiya, *The Church in the African American Experience* (Durham, N.C.: Duke University Press, 1990); Anne Streaty Wimberly, "A Black Christian Pedagogy of Hope: Religious Education in Black Perspective" (pp. 155-78), in *Forging a Better Religious Education in the Third Millennium*, ed. James Michael Lee (Birmingham, Ala.: Religious Education Press, 2000), 157.

5. Stephen L. Carter, *Integrity* (New York: BasicBooks, HarperCollins Publishers, 1996), 7.

6. See Carter, *Integrity*, 19-20.

7. This idea builds on Dwayne Huebner's posit that education is life's journey

that embraces the dimensions of our openness to the new and our constantly encountering the moreness and transforming potentials of life. See Vikki Hillis, ed., and William F. Pinar, collector, *The Lure of the Transcendent: Collected Essays by Dwayne E. Huebner* (Mahwah, N.J.: Lawrence Erlbaum Associates, 1999), 405.

8. Huebner makes a similar claim about the difficulties of life's journey and the propensity of life to present humans with questions for which no answer comes except "Continue on in faith." See ibid., 405. The words appear in the song "Just a Little Talk with Jesus," *The New National Baptist Hymnal* (Nashville: National Baptist Publishing Board, 1977), no. 298.

9. See ibid.

10. An extensive list of personal and corporate spiritual disciplines appears in Jenell Williams Paris and Margot Owen Eyring, *Urban Disciples: A Beginner's Guide to Serving God in the City* (Valley Forge, Pa.: Judson Press, 2000), 96-97.

11. Emily Herring Wilson, *Hope and Dignity: Older Black Women of the South* (Philadelphia: Temple University Press, 1983), 9.

12. Wilson, *Hope and Dignity*, 9.

13. Ibid.

14. Ibid.

15. Ibid., 9-10.

16. Mortimer J. Adler, *A Guidebook to Learning: For a Lifelong Pursuit of Wisdom* (New York: Macmillan Publishing Company, 1986), 111.

17. Ibid., 145.

18. Ibid., 115.

19. Ibid.

20. Cornel West draws on the significance of the reality of Jesus Christ, who, even in our finite Christian description, provides the basis for our struggle toward being fuller and faithful selves in Christ. He also draws on what he calls "the radical character" of Jesus' death and resurrection to make the claim that our staking our life on the decisive victory of Jesus Christ activates our hopeful attitude and choosing to live with hope. See Cornel West, *The Cornel West Reader* (New York: Basic *Civitas* Books, 1999), 419-20.

21. J. Glenn Gray, *The Promise of Wisdom: An Introduction to Philosophy of Education* (Philadelphia: Lippincott Company, 1968), 21.

22. See Charles F. Melchert, *Wise Teaching: Biblical Wisdom and Educational Ministry* (Harrisburg, Pa.: Trinity Press International, 1998), 138.

1. Forming Wisdom: Biblical and African Guides

1. See Paul J. Achtemeier, gen. ed., *Harper's Bible Dictionary* (San Francisco: Harper & Row, 1985), 1135.

2. Lawrence O. Richards, *Expository Dictionary of Bible Words* (Grand Rapids, Mich.: Regency Reference Library, Zondervan Publishing House, 1985), 629.

3. Roland E. Murphy, "Job, Book of," in *The Anchor Bible Dictionary*, vol. 6, ed. David Noel Freedman (New York: Doubleday Books, 1992), 922.

4. The bracketed feminine personal pronoun is inserted here from the Revised Standard Version of the Bible and is used to convey the sense of personification that heightens the impact of the message directed toward children as well as invites the children's close identification with the central character in the story.

5. Moshe Weinfeld, *Deuteronomy and the Deuteronomic School* (Oxford University Press, 1994), 133-54.

6. Gerhard von Rad, *The Problem of the Hexateuch and Other Essays* (New York: McGraw-Hill Book Company, 1966), 3-5.

7. G. Ernest Wright, "Deuteronomy," in *The Interpreter's Bible*, ed. G. A. Buttrick (New York: Abingdon Press, 1953), 484.

8. The Hebrew name for Ecclesiastes (taken from the Greek nomenclature) is Qoheleth, the speaker of the Assembly (Heb. *qahal*). For a discussion on the controversy of the name, see Roland E. Murphy, "Ecclesiastes, Book of," in *The Anchor Bible Dictionary*, vol. 2, ed. David Noel Freedman (New York: Doubleday Books, 1992), 271.

9. See James L. Mays, gen. ed., *Harper's Bible Commentary* (San Francisco: Harper & Row, 1988), 518, 520.

10. It is important to note that the phrase "All [this] is vanity and a chasing after wind" occurs six times in Ecclesiastes 1:12–6:9.

11. Mays, *Harper's Bible Commentary*, 524.

12. See also Tamba L. J. Mafico, "Tapping Our Roots: African and Biblical Teaching About Elders," in *Honoring African American Elders: A Ministry in the Soul Community*, ed. Anne Streaty Wimberly (San Francisco: Jossey-Bass Publishers, 1997), 28.

13. Africans depend on animals and birds to warn them of dangers that may lie ahead whenever they are on a long journey in a land with wild ferocious animals.

2. Forming Wisdom Through Cultural Rootedness

1. The Akan proverb is presented and discussed in Nsenga Warfield-Coppock, *Adolescent Rites of Passage*, vol. 1 of *Afrocentric Theory and Applications* (Washington, D.C.: Baobab Associates, 1990), 8.

2. Quoted from the school's information handout.

3. Paul Hill, Jr., *Coming of Age: African American Male Rites of Passage* (Chicago: African American Images, 1992), 66.

4. Cain Hope Felder, "Cultural Ideology, Afrocentrism, and Biblical Interpretation," in *Black Theology: A Documentary History, 1980–1992*, second edition, ed. James H. Cone and Gayraud S. Wilmore (Maryknoll: Orbis Books, 1993), 184.

5. Felder, "Cultural Ideology," 184-85.

6. Ibid., 188-91.

7. Amos N. Wilson, *Black-On-Black Violence: The Psychodynamics of Black Self-Annihilation in Service of White Domination* (New York: Afrikan World Infosystems, 1990), xii-xiii, 4-10.

8. Wilson, *Black-On-Black Violence*, 9.

9. Ibid., 9.

10. Ibid., 201-5.

11. Dr. Warren H. Stewart, Sr. used the term "triple heritage" to introduce his vision for an African American Christian Training School (AACTS), which he later established at the First Institutional Baptist Church of Phoenix, Arizona. AACTS is a Saturday school that provides a special program of study for children in kindergarten through tenth grade. The school has been in operation for approximately eight years and has a curriculum that emphasizes African, American, and Christian resources. My definition of the triple heritage differs slightly from the AACTS ministry in that I emphasize African American heritage

as the second component rather than American. For me, the term "African American" encompasses American heritage but also distinguishes the African American tradition within American culture. For purposes of this chapter, I use the term "black Americans" for the second component, in recognition of the larger group of Africans in the Diaspora in the United States.

12. Ali Alamin Mazrui also uses the term "triple heritage" in his book *The Africans: A Triple Heritage*. Mazrui describes the triple heritage as indigenous African traditions, Islamic culture, and Western civilization (p. 21). Mazrui engages in a critical analysis of Africa and of how the dynamics of the triple heritage have influenced the present condition of the motherland. Although these elements have contributed to numerous struggles in Africa, they also offer hope for her future. See Mazrui, *The Africans: A Triple Heritage* (Boston: Little, Brown and Company, 1986). Molefi Kete Asante and Hailu Habtu critique Mazrui, charging that his analysis of Africa is largely Eurocentric. They agree that Mazrui's study would benefit from an Afrocentric orientation. See Asante, *Kemet, Afrocentricity, and Knowledge* (Trenton: Africa World Press, 1990), 114-17; and Habtu, "The Fallacy of the 'Triple-Heritage' Thesis: A Critique," in *Issue* 13 (1984): 26-29.

13. Grant S. Shockley, "Black Pastoral Leadership in Religious Education: Social Justice Correlates," in *The Pastor as Religious Educator*, ed. Robert L. Browning (Birmingham: Religious Education Press, 1989), 178-209; idem "Christian Education and the Black Church," in *Christian Education Journey of Black Americans: Past, Present, Future*, comp. Charles Foster, Ethel R. Johnson, and Grant S. Shockley (Nashville: Discipleship Resources, 1985), 1-18; idem "Christian Education and the Black Religious Experience," in *Ethnicity in the Education of the Church*, ed. Charles R. Foster (Nashville: Scarritt Press, 1987), 29-47; idem "Historical Perspectives," in *Working with Black Youth: Opportunities for Christian Ministry*, ed. Charles Foster and Grant S. Shockley (Nashville: Abingdon Press, 1991), 9-29; idem "Religious Education and the Black Experience," in *The Black Church* 2, no. 1 (1972): 91-111.

14. Shockley, "Christian Education and the Black Church," 13.

15. Shockley, "Christian Education and the Black Church," 13-14; idem "From Emancipation to Transformation to Consummation: A Black Perspective," in *Does the Church Really Want Religious Education?: An Ecumenical Inquiry*, ed. Marlene Mayr (Birmingham: Religious Education Press, 1988), 241-42.

16. Shockley, "From Emancipation to Transformation," 225-28, 242-44.

17. Paul Nichols, "Blacks and the Religious Education Movement," in *Changing Patterns of Religious Education*, ed. Marvin J. Taylor (Nashville: Abingdon Press, 1984), 184-87.

18. Grant S. Shockley, "Black Theology," in *Harper's Encyclopedia of Religious Education*, ed. Iris V. Cully and Kendig Brubaker Cully (New York: Harper & Row, 1990), 80-82; idem, "Black Liberation, Christian Education and Black Social Indicators," *The Duke Divinity School Review* 40, no. 2 (1975): 109-25; idem, "Black Theology and Religious Education," in *Theologies of Religious Education*, ed. Randolph Crump Miller (Birmingham: Religious Education Press, 1995), 314-35; idem, "Liberation Theology, Black Theology, and Religious Education," in *Foundations for Christian Education in an Era of Change*, ed. Marvin J. Taylor (Nashville: Abingdon Press, 1976), 80-95.

19. Shockley, "Liberation Theology, Black Theology, and Religious Education," 86.

20. Shockley, "Christian Education and the Black Church," 15.

21. Ibid., 16-17.

22. Nichols, "Blacks and the Religious Education Movement," 190. See also my discussion of the relationship between black theology, womanist theology, and Christian education in "Womanist Hermeneutics: Implications for African American Christian Education," in *Womanist Biblical Hermeneutics*, ed. Mignon Jacobs (Pilgrim Press, forthcoming).

23. Shockley, "From Emancipation to Transformation," 244-46.

24. James H. Harris, "Christian Education: A Black Church Perspective," *Christian Ministry* (July-August 1991): 17.

25. Anne S. Wimberly, *Soul Stories: African American Christian Education* (Nashville: Abingdon Press, 1994), 13-14.

26. Wimberly, *Soul Stories*, 39.

27. Joseph V. Crockett, *Teaching Scripture from an African American Perspective* (Nashville: Discipleship Resources, 1990), xii.

28. Crockett, *Teaching Scripture from an African American Perspective*, 1-2, 15-17, 27-31, 39-41.

29. Nsenga Warfield-Coppock, *Adolescent Rites of Passage*, vol. 1 of *Afrocentric Theory and Applications* (Washington, D.C.: Baobab Associates, 1990), 8.

30. Janice E. Hale, "The Transmission of Faith to Young African American Children," in *The Recovery of Black Presence: An Interdisciplinary Exploration*, ed. Randall C. Bailey and Jacquelyn Grant (Nashville: Abingdon Press, 1995), 193.

31. Hale, "The Transmission of Faith to Young African American Children," 193.

32. Peter J. Paris, *The Spirituality of African Peoples: The Search for a Common Moral Discourse* (Minneapolis: Fortress Press, 1995), 20.

33. I introduce this model in my chapter "Womanist Hermeneutics: Implications for African American Christian Education," in *Womanist Biblical Hermeneutics*. The current discussion of the model differs slightly in that this chapter refers to the components of the triple heritage as African, black American, and Christian rather than African, African American, and Christian. This chapter recognizes the diverse group of Africans in the Diaspora as well as those from the Caribbean, Bermuda, Britain, and African countries who reside in the United States. Also, in this chapter I discuss the triple-heritage model specifically in regards to its usefulness in wisdom formation efforts in the black churches' educational ministry, whereas in the previously identified chapter on womanist hermeneutic, I introduce the model from my perspective as a womanist religious educator.

34. A version of the spiritual appears in *Songs of Zion* (Nashville: Abingdon Press, 1981), 106.

35. Zora Neale Hurston, "Spirituals and Neo-Spirituals," in *The Negro in Music and Art*, ed. Lindsay Patterson (1933; reprint, New York: Publishers Company, 1967), 15.

36. The words appear in the song "I've Got a Robe," which is found in *Songs of Zion*, no. 82.

37. A version of the song "Go Down Moses" is found in *Songs of Zion*, no. 112.

38. Jon Michael Spencer, *Protest and Praise: Sacred Music of Black Religion* (Minneapolis: Fortress Press, 1990), 13.

39. Mary Elizabeth Moore, "Rhythmic Curriculum: Guiding an Educative Journey" (a paper presented in the symposium Les Rythmes Educatifs dans la Philosophie de Whitehead, Universite Catholique de Lille, Lille, France, April 25-27, 1994), 19-20.

3. Forming Wisdom Through Cross-generational Connectedness

1. Birmingham is the second largest city in England, with a population of approximately 1.2 million people. Birmingham has the largest concentration of people of African heritage, after London. My work has been undertaken with African Caribbean children and young people and their families in predominantly poor inner-city areas in the city.

2. This work with Caribbean young people in England resulted in the first African-centered approach to Christian education in England. The approach is published in Anthony G. Reddie, *Growing into Hope*, vols. 1 and 2 (Peterborough: The Methodist Publishing House, 1998). See also Anthony G. Reddie, "Towards a Black Christian Education of Liberation: The Christian Education of Black Children in Britain," in *Black Theology in Britain: A Journal of Contextual Praxis*, no. 1 (1998): 46-58; Anthony G. Reddie, "The Case for a Contextualised Christian Education for Black Children and Young People in Britain: A Survey of the Literature," *A Black Theology Journal of Contextual Praxis*, no. 3 (1999): 66-78; Anthony G. Reddie, "The Oral Tradition of African Caribbean People as Resources for Black Christian Formation," *British Journal of Theological Education*, vol. 10 (Summer 1998): 16-25.

3. Fred Lofton, "Teaching Christian Values Within the Family," in *The Black Family: Past, Present, and Future*, ed. June N. Lee (Grand Rapids, Mich.: Zondervan Publishing, 1991), 127.

4. Colleen Birchett, "A History of Religious Education in the Black Church," in *Urban Church Education*, ed. Donald B. Rogers (Birmingham, Ala.: Religious Education Press, 1989), 74.

5. Grant Shockley, "From Emancipation to Transformation to Consummation: A Black Perspective," in *Does the Church Really Want Religious Education?* ed. Marlene Mayr (Birmingham, Ala.: Religious Education Press, 1989), 236.

6. Ella P. Mitchell, "Oral Tradition: The Legacy of Faith for the Black Church," *Religious Education*, vol. 81 (Winter 1986): 93-112.

7. See Anthony G. Reddie, *Growing into Hope: Liberation and Change*, vol. 2 (Peterborough: The Methodist Publishing House, 1998), 15-38.

8. Reddie, *Growing into Hope*, vol. 2, 15.

9. Ibid., 18-20.

10. See Kwesi Owusu, ed., *Black British Culture and Society* (London: Routledge, 2000); Peter Fryer, *Staying Power: The History of Black People in Britain* (London: Pluto Press, 1992); and Ron Ramdin, *Reimaging Britain: 500 Years of Black and Asian History* (London: Pluto Press, 1999).

11. Molefi Kente Asante, "Afrocentricity and Culture," in *The Rhythms of Unity*, ed. Molefi Kente Asante and Kariamu Welsh Asante (Trenton, N.J.: Africa World Press, 1990), 4.

4. Singing Hope in the Key of Wisdom: Wisdom Formation of Youth

1. Thomas A. Dorsey, "The Lord Will Make a Way Somehow," *The New National Baptist Hymnal* (Nashville: National Baptist Publishing Board, 1977), no. 286.

2. Michael Dyson asserts that there is a gulf between the hip-hop generation and the older generations that results from the hip-hop generation's " 'stylistic conflict' and ideological agendas." See Michael Eric Dyson, *Between God and Gangsta Rap: Bearing Witness to Black Culture* (New York: Oxford University Press, 1996), xiii.

3. Dorsey, "The Lord Will Make A Way Somehow."

4. *Songs of Zion* (Nashville: Abingdon Press, 1981), no. 86.

5. Charles Foster and Grant S. Shockley, *Working with Black Youth: Opportunities for Christian Ministry* (Nashville: Abingdon Press, 1989), 9.

6. Ibid., 12.

7. Ibid, 3.

8. Evelyn Parker, *Twenty Seeds of Hope: Religious-Moral Values in African American Adolescents in Chicagoland and Implications for Christian Education in the Black Church* (Ph.D. diss., Northwestern University, 1996), 71.

9. Foster and Shockley, *Working with Black Youth*, 23.

10. Ibid., 26.

11. Grant S. Shockley, "Ultimatum and Hope" (National Committee of Negro Churchmen Convocation and the Black Church Movement), *Christian Century* 86 (Fall 1969): 217-19.

12. Earl L. Steward, *African American Music* (New York: Schirmer Books, 1998), 66. Steward quotes theomusicologist Jon Michael Spencer, *Black Hymnody: A Hymnological History of the African-American Church* (Knoxville: University of Tennessee Press, 1992), 36.

13. Ibid., 65.

14. Ibid., 80.

15. Steward, *African American Music*, 252.

16. Ibid., 264.

17. Ibid., 265.

18. Ibid.

19. Kirk Franklin, biography, www.nunation.com.

20. Kirk Franklin et al., "Stomp" (Remix). Lilly Mack Music, 1997.

21. Ibid.

22. Kirk Franklin, "My Life Is in Your Hands," Lilly Mack Music, 1996.

23. I concur with Teresa Fry Brown's definition of the proverb "Trouble don't last always." I acknowledge her argument that hope means perseverance, but I also include expectation and agency.

24. Mary Mary, *Thankful*, biography, http://www.mary-mary.com.

25. Ibid.

26. Mary Mary, *Thankful*. These words are a translation of rapper on CD and not printed.

27. Mary, Mary, *Thankful* (2001).

28. The song appears in *Songs of Zion*, no. 72.

29. For a discussion of the spirituals and Burleigh's arrangement of them, see *Spirituals of Harry T. Burleigh* (Melville, N.Y.: Belwin-Mills Publishing Corp., 1984), 4.

30. Ibid., 129-32.

31. *Songs of Zion*, no. 175.

32. Mary Mary, "Can't Give Up Now," from their *Thankful* album (2000).

33. James Cone, *Black Theology and Black Power* (San Francisco: Harper & Row, 1969), 123.

34. Ibid., 123.

35. Dyson, *Between God and Gangsta Rap*, 137-38.

36. Peter Parish indicates that the communal value is most prominent among African and African Americans in *The Spirituality of African Peoples: The Search for a Common Moral Discourse* (Minneapolis, Minn.: Fortress Press, 1995).

37. Cheryl Kirk-Duggan writes about lamenting in teenagers in a forthcoming publication on spiritual practices for today's teens.

5. Counsel from Wise Others: Forming Wisdom Through Male Mentoring

1. See Frank B. Stanger, *Spiritual Formation in the Local Church* (Grand Rapids: Zondervan Publishing House, 1989), 17.

2. Trunell D. Felder, *An Inward Outward Journey: A Paradigm for the Spiritual Formation of the African American Male Disciple*, A Doctor of Ministry Dissertation (Atlanta: Interdenominational Theological Center, 2000), 5-6.

3. Theodore M. Newcomb and Everett K. Wilson, *College Peer Groups* (Chicago: Aldine Publishing Company, 1966), 11.

4. Ibid., 11.

5. Ibid., 13.

6. A complete description of the session in which the men disclosed these characteristics appears in Felder, *An Inward Outward Journey*, 82-83.

7. Geoff Peruniak, "Helping Adults Learn," interview with Dr. Laurent A. Daloz on his book *Effective Teaching and Mentoring: Realizing the Transformational Power of Adult Learning Experiences* (Oxford: Jossey-Bass Publishers, 1990), http://aurora.icaap.org/archive/daloz.html.

8. Felder, *An Inward Outward Journey*, 124.

9. Edward P. Wimberly, *Relational Refugees: Alienation and Reincorporation in African American Churches and Communities* (Nashville: Abingdon Press, 2000), 33.

10. Felder, *An Inward Outward Journey*, 124.

11. See Rodney J. Hunter, *Dictionary of Pastoral Care and Counseling* (Nashville: Abingdon Press, 1990), 571.

12. Felder, *An Inward Outward Journey*, 90.

13. Kelsey's view appears in: Peter C. Hodgson and Robert King, *Christian Theology: An Introduction to Its Traditions and Tasks* (Philadelphia: Fortress Press, 1985), 177.

14. Luke T. Johnson, *The Writings of the New Testament: An Interpretation* (Philadelphia: Fortress Press, 1986), 334.

15. Felder, *An Inward Outward Journey*, 4-5.

16. Ibid., 65.

17. Ibid., 65, 100, 114-15.

18. Anne Streaty Wimberly, *Soul Stories: African American Christian Education* (Nashville: Abingdon Press, 1994), 25.

19. In her discussion on the ecclesia, Rebecca Chopp refers to the kind of shift in rules, categories, visions, and relations that renews community as "emancipatory transformation." I am suggesting here that the same kind of shift is necessary with black males and must be a goal of wisdom-forming mentoring processes with these males. See Rebecca Chopp, *The Power to Speak: Feminism, Language, and God* (New York: Crossroad Books, 1991), 76.

20. See Jim Wilhoit, *Christian Education and the Search for Meaning* (Grand Rapids: Baker Book House, 1986), 60.

6. Conversations on Word and Deed: Forming Wisdom Through Female Mentoring

1. Katie G. Cannon, *Black Womanist Ethics* (Atlanta: Scholars Press, 1988); Katie G. Cannon, *Katie's Canon* (New York: Continuum Books, 1995).
2. Emilie M. Townes, *Womanist Justice, Womanist Hope* (Atlanta: Scholars Press, 1993); Emilie M. Townes, *In a Blaze of Glory* (Nashville: Abingdon Press, 1995).
3. N. Lynne Westfield, *Dear Sisters: A Womanist Practice of Hospitality* (Cleveland: The Pilgrim Press, 2001).
4. Delores S. Williams, *Sisters in the Wilderness: The Challenge of Womanist God-Talk* (Maryknoll, N.Y.: Orbis Books, 1993).
5. Emilie M. Townes, ed., *A Troubling in My Soul: Womanist Perspectives on Evil and Suffering* (Maryknoll, N.Y.: Orbis Books, 1993).
6. See Renita J. Weems, *Just a Sister Away: A Womanist Vision of Women's Relationships in the Bible* (San Diego: LuraMedia, 1988), x; and Westfield, *Dear Sisters*, 40-103.
7. Cannon, *Black Womanist Ethics*, 4; Weems, *Just a Sister Away*, x.
8. Townes, *In a Blaze of Glory*, 10.
9. Margo Murray with Marna A. Owens, *Beyond the Myths and Magic of Mentoring* (San Francisco: Jossey-Bass Publishers, 1991), 5.
10. A similar outcome is identified in the functioning of encounter groups described in Sidney M. Jourard, "A Way to Encounter," in *Confrontation: Encounters in Self and Interpersonal Awareness*, 107-19, ed. Leonard Blank, Gloria B. Gottsegen, and Monroe G. Gottsegen (New York: The Macmillan Company, 1971), 110.
11. This womanist approach builds on the burgeoning literature set forth by black women that focuses on the distinctive experiences of black women in racist, sexist, oppressive society and black women's resistance to these societal realities. The term "womanist" also derives from the descriptive definition appearing in Alice Walker, *In Search of Our Mothers' Gardens: Womanist Prose* (San Diego: Harcourt Brace Jovanovich, 1983), xi.
12. See Jacquelyn Grant, *White Women's Christ and Black Women's Jesus: Feminist Christology and Womanist Response* (Atlanta: Scholars Press, 1989), 209-18.
13. Ibid., 205.
14. See Gale Kennebrew-Moore, "Releasing the Womanist Song," in *WomanistCare: How to Tend the Souls of Women*, ed. Linda H. Hollies, (Joliet, Ill.: Woman to Woman Ministries Publication, 1992); Teresa E. Snorton, "The Legacy of the African-American Matriarch: New Perspectives for Pastoral Care," in *Through the Eyes of Women: Insights for Pastoral Care*, 50-65, ed. Jeanne Stevenson Moessner (Minneapolis: Fortress Press, 1996); Teresa E. Snorton, "Self-Care for the African American Woman," in *In Her Own Time: Women and Developmental Issues in Pastoral Care*, ed. Jeanne Stevenson-Moessner (Minneapolis: Fortress Press, 2000).
15. Westfield, *Dear Sisters*, 40-52.
16. Anthony J. Gittins, *Gifts and Strangers* (New York: Paulist Press, 1989), 91-108.

7. Wisdom Formation in Middle and Late Adulthood

1. Howard Thurman, *Deep Is the Hunger: Meditations for Apostles of Sensitiveness* (Richmond, Ind.: Friends United Press, 1951) , 11, 12, 13.

2. See Evelyn E. Whitehead and James D. Whitehead, *Christian Life Patterns: The Psychological Challenges and Religious Invitations of Adult Life* (New York: Doubleday, 1979); and Evelyn E. Whitehead and James D. Whitehead, *Marrying Well: Stages on the Journey of Christian Marriage* (Garden City, N.Y.: Doubleday, 1981), 249-50.

3. Thurman, *Deep Is the Hunger*, 16-17.

4. Janice Ruffin, "Stages of Adult Development in Black Professional Women," in *Black Adult Development and Aging*, ed. Reginald Jones (Berkeley, Calif.: Cobb and Henry, 1989), 31-62.

5. Winston Gooden, "Development of Black Men in Early Adulthood," in ibid., 63-90.

6. Paul Ricoeur, *The Symbolism of Evil* (Boston: Beacon Press, 1967), 351-52.

7. Erik Erikson, *Childhood and Society* (New York: W.W. Norton, 1963).

8. Anne Streaty Wimberly, *Soul Stories: African American Christian Education* (Nashville: Abingdon Press, 1994), 95.

9. Pearl Cleage, *I Wish I Had a Red Dress* (New York: William Morrow, 2001), 23.

10. Ibid., 27.

11. Sylvia Ann Hewlett and Cornel West, *The War Against Parents: What We Can Do for America's Beleaguered Moms and Dads* (New York: Houghton Mifflin, 1998), 30.

12. Colleen Leahy Johnson, "Active and Latent Functions of Grandparenting During the Divorce Process," *The Gerontologist*, 28 (2), (1988): 188.

13. The historical obligatory rather than voluntary role of black grandmothers was documented in the early work of E. Franklin Frazier, *The Negro Family in the United States* (Chicago: University of Chicago Press, 1939); and in the more recent work of Richard W. Owens, *The Impact of African-American Grandparents' Involvement/Role in Family Structure: A Content Analysis Study of Professional Social Science Journals* (unpublished doctoral diss., Atlanta: Clark University, 1994); Anne Streaty Wimberly, "From Intercessory Hope to Mutual Intercession: Grandparents Raising Grandchildren and the Church's Response," *Family Ministry: Empowering Through Faith* 14 (3), (Fall 2000): 19-37.

14. Wimberly, "From Intercessory Hope to Mutual Intercession," 20.

15. Ibid., 30-35.

16. Cleage, *I Wish I Had a Red Dress*, 25.

17. Terry D. Hargrave, *Families and Forgiveness: Healing Wounds in the Intergenerational Family* (New York: Brunner/Mazel Publishers, 1994), 218.

18. Richard C. Osmer, "Education, Nurture, and Care," *Dictionary of Pastoral Care and Counseling*, 336-38, ed. Rodney J. Hunter (Nashville: Abingdon Press, 1990), 337.

19. Brian H. Childs, "Forgiveness," *Dictionary of Pastoral Care and Counseling,* ed. Rodney J. Hunter (Nashville: Abingdon Press, 1990), 439.

20. Thomas emphasizes the joyful and exuberant nature of celebratory black worship in Frank A. Thomas, *They Like to Never Quit Praisin' God: The Role of Celebration in Preaching* (Cleveland: United Church Press, 1997), 5.

21. Washington uses the phrase "an oratory of hope" to describe the function of prayer in black religion. His discussion of the phrase appears in James Melvin

Washington, ed., *Conversations with God: Two Centuries of Prayers by African Americans* (New York: HarperCollins Publishers, 1994), xxx.

22. See Anne Streaty Wimberly, ed., *Honoring African American Elders: A Ministry in the Soul Community* (San Francisco: Jossey-Bass Publishers, 1997), 8.

23. Arnold van Gennep, *Rites of Passage* (Chicago: University of Chicago Press, 1960), 10-11.

24. Ruby Dee and Ossie Davis, "A Lasting Love," *The African American Book of Values*, ed. Steven Barboza (New York: Doubleday, Bantam Doubleday Dell Publishing Group, Inc., 1998), 657.

25. Dee and Davis, "A Lasting Love," 657.

26. Edith Dalton Thomas, Anne Streaty Wimberly, and Edward P. Wimberly, "Honoring and Sharing Our Elder's Wisdom," in Wimberly, *Honoring African American Elders*, 172.

8. The Formation of Wisdom and Human Sexuality

1. Howard Thurman, *Meditations of the Heart* (Richmond, Ind.: Friends United Press, 1976; reprint of the 1953 edition published by Harper & Row, New York), 207.

2. Loretta Sweet Jemmott and her associates make the point that "it is important to understand the nature of African American religious affiliations because they provide an insight into sources of support, social networks, and potential organizing structures for prevention activities . . .[and] for understanding the values and norms in African American communities." This view is found in Loretta Sweet Jemmott, John B. Jemmott III, Katherine Hutchinson, "HIV/AIDS," in *Health Issues in the Black Community*, ed. Ronald L. Braithwaite and Sandra E. Taylor, 309-46 (San Francisco: Jossey-Bass Publishers, 2001), 329.

3. June Dobbs Butts, "Sex Therapy, Intimacy, and the Role of the Black Physician in the AIDS Era," *Journal of the National Medical Association*, 80 (1988): 919-22.

4. Edward P. Wimberly, "Pastoral Care of Sexual Diversity in the Black Church," *American Journal of Pastoral Counseling*, 3, 3/4, (2001): 45-58.

5. Peter L. Berger and Thomas Luckmann, *The Social Construction of Reality: A Treatise in the Sociology of Knowledge* (Garden City, N.Y.: Anchor Books, 1967), 49.

6. Ibid., 50.

7. David F. Greenberg, *The Construction of Homosexuality* (Chicago: University of Chicago Press, 1988).

8. William R. Stayton, "Faith-based Sexuality: Educational Programs That Work," *CSR Connections*, 2 (Spring 2001): 4-10.

9. Ibid., 4.

10. Jemmott, Jemmott, and Hutchinson, "HIV/AIDS," 310.

11. Ibid., 311.

12. Ibid., 310-11.

13. Alwyn T. Cohall and Hope E. Bannister, "The Health Status of Children and Adolescents," in *Health Issues in the Black Community*, 2d ed., ed. Ronald L. Braithwaite and Sandra E. Taylor, 13-43 (San Francisco: Jossey-Bass Publishers, 2001), 22-23.

14. Jemmott, Jemmott, and Hutchinson, "HIV/AIDS," 312-13.

15. Ibid., 312-14.

16. David. S. Schnarch, *Constructing the Sexual Crucible: An Integration of Sexual and Marital Therapy* (New York: W.W. Norton, 1991), 261.

17. The following novels are the bases for the comments being made: E. Lynn Harris, *Invisible Life* (New York: Anchor Books, 1991); *Just As I Am* (New York: Anchor Books, 1994); *And This Too Shall Pass* (New York: Anchor Books, 1996); *If This World Were Mine* (New York: Anchor Books, 1998); *Abide with Me* (New York: Anchor Books, 2000); *Not a Day Goes By* (New York: Doubleday, 2000).

18. Pearl Cleage, *What Looks Like Crazy on an Ordinary Day* (New York: Anchor Books, 1997).

19. See "Fact Sheet: Faith Communities and HIV/AIDS," http://aawhworldhealth.org/WAD99/fs_faith.html.

20. Louise D. Palmer, "Faith-based Sex Education Takes Hold in Churches, Temples Across U.S.," Newhouse News Service 2000. Reprinted at http://www.uua.org/news/owl/newhouse5500.html

21. Palmer, "Faith-based Sex Education Takes Hold in Churches, Temples Across U.S.," 2.

22. Ibid., 3.

9. Forming a Spirituality of Wisdom

1. Michael I. N. Dash, Jonathan Jackson, and Stephen C. Rasor, *Hidden Wholeness: An African American Spirituality for Individuals and Communities* (Cleveland: United Church Press, 1997), 4.

2. Ibid., 38.

3. In addition to focusing on the communal dimension of spirituality in Dash, Jackson, and Rasor, *Hidden Wholeness*, Jamie Phelps also explores the dimension of communal character in the spirituality of black people in Jamie Phelps, "Black Spirituality," in *Spiritual Traditions for the Contemporary Church*, ed. Robin Maas and Gabriel O'Donnell (Nashville: Abingdon Press, 1990), 332-33.

4. References to de Mello and a version of the story appear in Dash, Jackson, and Rasor, *Hidden Wholeness*, xvii-xviii. See also quotations from Anthony de Mello, http://www.gurteen.com/gurteen/gurteen.nsf.

5. Dash, Jackson, and Rasor, *Hidden Wholeness*, xvi.

6. Ibid., 108.

7. Ibid.

8. Ibid.

9. From *The Book of Common Prayer* (New York: The Seabury Press, 1979), 718.

10. See Jamie Phelps, "Black Spirituality," 342.

11. Dash, Jackson, and Rasor, *Hidden Wholeness*, 110.

12. Ibid.

13. Thomas Merton, *New Seeds of Contemplation* (New York: New Directions Books, 1962), 155-56.

14. Ibid., 156.

15. Ibid.

16. Lawrence O. Richards, *Expository Dictionary of Bible Words* (Grand Rapids, Mich.: Regency Reference Library, Zondervan Publishing House, 1985), 598.

17. Dash, Jackson, and Rasor, *Hidden Wholeness*, 40.

18. See Dash, Jackson, and Rasor, *Hidden Wholeness*, 55; and Cornel West, *Race Matters* (Boston: Beacon Press, 1993), 14-15.

19. See Dash, Jackson, and Rasor, *Hidden Wholeness*, 120-21.

20. A similar understanding of wisdom is embraced by the Apache Indians in the western United States. This conception appears in: Keith H. Basso, *Wisdom Sits in Places: Landscape and Language Among the Western Apache* (Albuquerque: University of New Mexico Press, 1996), 127.

21. The activities included here are based largely on ones appearing in Dash, Jackson, and Rasor, *Hidden Wholeness*, 134, 135, 138.

Contributors

Trunell D. Felder, D.Min., is senior pastor of New Faith Baptist Church in Matteson, Illinois.

Maisha I. Handy, Ph.D., is assistant professor of Christian education at Interdenominational Theological Center, Atlanta, Georgia.

Jonathan Jackson, Jr., Th.D., prior to his death on March 12, 2002, was the director of the Interdenominational Theological Center Faith and the City Project, and professor emeritus of Christian education at that institution, where he also served as chairperson of the Academic Area called The Church and Its Ministries (CAM). He is coauthor of *Hidden Wholeness: An African American Spirituality for Individuals and Communities*.

Temba L. J. Mafico, Ph.D., is professor of Old Testament and biblical Hebrew and associate dean of academic affairs at Interdenominational Theological Center in Atlanta, Georgia. He has published articles in the *Anchor Bible Dictionary*, the *Journal of Theology for Southern Africa*, and the *Journal of Northwest Semitic Languages*.

Evelyn L. Parker, Ph.D., is assistant professor of Christian education at Perkins School of Theology at Southern Methodist University in Dallas, Texas. She has published a chapter in *Thinking Theologically About Youth Ministry*, edited by Kenda Creasy Dean, Chap Clark, and Dave Rahn.

Anthony G. Reddie, Ph.D., is research fellow at the Queens Foundation for Ecumenical Theological Education in

Birmingham, England, and research consultant in Christian education and development for the British Methodist Church. He is the author of the two-volume work entitled *Growing into Hope.*

Yolanda Y. Smith, Ph.D., is assistant professor of Christian education at Yale University Divinity School, New Haven, Connecticut. She coedited *Resources for Sacred Teaching* and chapters in *Faith of Our Foremothers.*

Anne Streaty Wimberly, Ph.D., is professor of Christian education and director of the Youth Hope-Builders Academy and Ecumenical Families Alive Project at Interdenominational Theological Center in Atlanta, Georgia. She is author of *Soul Stories: African American Christian Education, The Church Family Sings*, as well as editor and contributing author of *Honoring African American Elders: A Ministry in the Soul Community.*

Edward P. Wimberly, Ph.D., is executive vice president and dean of academic services at Interdenominational Theological Center in Atlanta, Georgia, where he also is Jarena Lee Professor of Pastoral Care and Counseling. His recent publications include *Counseling African American Marriages and Families* and *Relational Refugees: Alienation and Reincorporation in African American Churches and Communities.*